Cambridge Elements

Elements in the Philosophy of Biology
edited by
Grant Ramsey
KU Leuven

THE ORGANISM

Jan Baedke
Ruhr University Bochum

Shaftesbury Road, Cambridge CB2 8EA, United Kingdom

One Liberty Plaza, 20th Floor, New York, NY 10006, USA

477 Williamstown Road, Port Melbourne, VIC 3207, Australia

314–321, 3rd Floor, Plot 3, Splendor Forum, Jasola District Centre,
New Delhi – 110025, India

103 Penang Road, #05-06/07, Visioncrest Commercial, Singapore 238467

Cambridge University Press is part of Cambridge University Press & Assessment,
a department of the University of Cambridge.

We share the University's mission to contribute to society through the pursuit of
education, learning and research at the highest international levels of excellence.

www.cambridge.org
Information on this title: www.cambridge.org/9781009495059

DOI: 10.1017/9781009495035

First published 2025

A catalogue record for this publication is available from the British Library

ISBN 978-1-009-49505-9 Hardback
ISBN 978-1-009-49506-6 Paperback
ISSN 2515-1126 (online)
ISSN 2515-1118 (print)

Cambridge University Press & Assessment has no responsibility for the persistence or
accuracy of URLs for external or third-party internet websites referred to in this
publication and does not guarantee that any content on such websites is, or will
remain, accurate or appropriate.

For EU product safety concerns, contact us at Calle de José Abascal, 56, 1°, 28003
Madrid, Spain, or email eugpsr@cambridge.org

The Organism

Elements in the Philosophy of Biology

DOI: 10.1017/9781009495035
First published online: June 2025

Jan Baedke
Ruhr University Bochum

Author for correspondence: Jan Baedke, jan.baedke@rub.de

Abstract: Organisms are central for biology. However, conceptualizing the unit of the organism is not easy. This Element discusses challenges to base biological reasoning and practice on the concept of organism. After many decades dominated by the paradigm of the gene, the organism is making a comeback in the bio- and biomedical sciences. It is again recognized as a causally efficacious, autonomous, and active unit that transcends the properties of genes and affects its own development and evolution – especially in fields like epigenetics, niche construction theory, and evolutionary developmental biology. This Element investigates these developments from a perspective of integrated history and philosophy of science. It focuses on conceptual, biotheoretical, and historical dimensions, as well as sociopolitical and anthropological aspects of today's 'return of the organism.' In particular, it discusses solutions for challenges of organism-centered biosciences in the 21st century. This title is also available as Open Access on Cambridge Core.

Keywords: organism, life, biological individuality, agency, organicism

ISBNs: 9781009495059 (HB), 9781009495066 (PB), 9781009495035 (OC)
ISSNs: 2515-1126 (online), 2515-1118 (print)

Contents

1 Introduction

It seems like a truism that biologists study organisms. But not every scientist or philosopher is convinced by this idea. For instance, developmental biologist Brian Goodwin (1999, 239) once observed: "Organisms have disappeared as fundamental entities, as basic unities, from contemporary biology because they have no real status as centres of causal agency." He lamented that organisms "are now considered to be generated by the genes they contain" and thus lack causal efficacy themselves.

This Element will show that, indeed, several deep tensions underlie biology's understanding of organisms. Organisms surely matter in various fields, from ecology, behavioral biology, and developmental biology to evolutionary biology, but, at the same time, identifying and conceptualizing this very unit is anything but easy. In the history of biology, this ambiguity has led many biologists to search for other units that seemingly could be grasped more easily to guide their reasoning and practices. In recent times, the central unit has been the gene. But while the 20th century can be labeled the 'century of the gene' (Keller 2000), in the past three decades, attempts have been made to establish an 'organism-centered biology' once again. Recent calls for the 'return of the organism' have been stirred through new findings in fields such as evolutionary developmental biology (Evo-Devo), epigenetics, microbiome research, and niche construction theory. In these fields, researchers have worked to reestablish the organism as a central explanatory unit in biology – one that structures reasoning about and investigations of living systems, such as how they interact with their environment, develop, reproduce, and evolve.

With this reemerging interest in the organism, long-standing and unresolved philosophical issues reemerge: In the first place, what elements of nature are part of the unit of the organism? What kind of biological individual is the organism that legitimizes its allegedly special causal status? Are organisms agents? How should we conceptualize the organism–environment relation? How can we rightfully say that organism-centered explanations of a particular biological phenomenon are better than gene-centered ones? What consequence does this shift in perspective have on understanding ourselves as human beings, and on how we relate to our environment and to one another? And: What biomedical consequences does the new emphasis on organismal development and organism–environment relations have? The aim of this Element is to carve a way through these difficult biophilosophical and socio-anthropological issues. This endeavor is guided by three bundles of questions:

(i) Which theoretical positions in the history of biology have defended the view that the concept of organism should be the explanatory starting point of biology? What can we learn from them?

(ii) How can biology be rooted theoretically on the unit of the organism? Which kind of conceptualization of the organism is needed for that? What challenges does it face?

(iii) How does an organism-centered biology shape our view of ourselves as human beings?

These three sets of questions are interrelated. The historical analysis should not only provide an understanding of past attempts to orient biology (and especially evolutionary biology) toward organism-centeredness, but rather bring to light problems these accounts faced when conceptualizing the organism, which still matter today. Against the background of stimulating past conceptual frameworks, these long-standing and unsolved conceptual and theoretical challenges will be addressed philosophically. This also includes discussing which socially and anthropologically relevant discourses are affected by (and affect) the conceptual framework of organism-centered biology, especially how we understand ourselves and relate to our material and social environment. In this sense, this Element adopts a perspective of integrated history and philosophy of science (&HPS), augmented by considerations of the sociocultural dimensions of science.

The Element's agenda is as follows: It first (Section 2) introduces the history of the organism concept from the 17th century to the 'eclipse of the organism' during the 20th century. Against the background of this history, the organism concept is understood as a 'nexus concept.' It serves as a core interface that interlinks epistemic and ontological aspects of various concepts, like life, organization, and teleology, making it highly versatile in biological research but also difficult to grasp.

Second (Section 3), this Element provides an overview of recent empirical findings in postgenomics and biomedicine, and in fields like Evo-Devo, epigenetics, niche construction theory, and microbiome research that stir attempts to revive the organism concept. It also discusses recent philosophical debates on biological individuality and teleology that are informative for how to individuate organisms and to understand their activities and agential behaviors. I will argue that there are two long-standing challenges for organism-centered biology linked to the question of how to conceptualize organisms: The 'inward challenge,' which deals with the question of what the internal organization of the organism is that distinguishes it from other biological units; and the 'outward challenge,' which concerns how we can separate organisms from their environment (especially if we recognize that organisms can actively construct their environment and thus are inextricably interlinked with it). I argue that these two challenges need to be addressed to understand how organisms affect developmentally, ecologically and evolutionary relevant causal pathways *inside of them* and *in their environment.*

In Section 4, the history of these two challenges will be explored by focusing on debates in early theoretical biology and philosophy of biology in the first half of the 20th century – in intellectual movements like organicism, holistic biology, and dialectical materialism. This Element will first introduce the reader to these movements and their approaches toward conceptualizing the organism and establishing an organism-centered biology. Then, I explore how they addressed the 'inward' and 'outward challenge' and discuss their proposed theoretical solutions. However, as I will argue, these solutions faced important shortcomings which resurface in today's 'return of the organism.' This concerns, for example, an overemphasis on concepts like self-maintenance and persistence to clarify the internal organization of organisms, which limits our understanding of the creative and agential forms in which organisms can reorganize and change themselves in new ways; or the tendency to blur or neglect boundaries between reciprocally interacting organisms and environments, which makes it impossible to identify the organism. I will suggest a new conceptualization of the organism that can overcome these problematic trends. It allows not only to unambiguously individuate the organism but also to highlight its crucial epistemic role as an active and creative agent in developmental evolution.

In Section 5, I explore sociopolitical and anthropological dimensions of the organism concept. How we define us as individual organisms and our boundaries deeply affects our social relations. I provide an overview of how current postgenomic developments in biomedicine lead to views of self-determination and autonomy of individuals but also of environmental determinism and social heteronomy. In addition, I discuss how new debates about the organism draw on racial classifications (e.g., in epigenetics and microbiome research) for studying disease susceptibilities of environmentally embedded individuals. Against the background of past sociopolitical agendas that built on organismal frameworks, for example, in the early 20th century, I conclude that we should be skeptical of the assumption that a move from the gene to the organism (and toward organismal plasticity and agency) necessarily will go along with liberal sociopolitical agendas that highlight humans' autonomy and freedom. An organism-centered biology is also compatible with deterministic, exclusionary and racist views on human individuals.

I conclude (Section 6) by highlighting the need for historians and philosophers of science, as well as biologists, to gain a deeper understanding of old challenges concerning the organism concept, to improve the conceptual and theoretical precision and depth necessary for solving these problems, and to raise more awareness of sociopolitical agendas underlying organism-centered biology in the 21st century.

2 The History of the Organism Concept: A Nexus in Biology

The concept of the organism has a rich and multifaced history. It began to appear in biological texts in the late 17th century (Cheung 2006, 2014).[1] The vitalist physician Georg Ernst Stahl (1684) first coined the term to describe the purposeful organization of a living body. In the wake of heated debates between mechanists and vitalists, Stahl highlighted the organism as the principle that distinguishes living systems from machines. He, in fact, applied the concept not only to natural beings but also to man-made apparatuses and acknowledged that many phenomena in living bodies involve mechanical movement. However, unlike mechanical bodies, organisms have an internal order and orientation of parts working toward a common goal. He attributes this order to an internal principle that directs, governs, and controls the organism, with the ultimate purpose of preserving the body.

This early characterization introduced several ideas that became influential for biological reasoning about organisms, especially from a physiological perspective. Following Stahl, biologists and natural philosophers often conceptualized the organism as a *living unit* of *interacting parts* that *preserves its order or organization and thus itself* and that is *oriented toward a final purpose*. The organism thus draws on several other concepts, that of life, parthood and part–whole relations, preservation and self-maintenance, (self-)organization, as well as intrinsic purposiveness and teleology.

We may thus describe 'organism' as a *nexus concept*: a concept that forms a core or interface in which epistemic and ontological facets of other concepts can be interlinked and connected in different ways (see Box 1). This characteristic makes the organism concept highly versatile within biological research. In fact, in the history of biology it has stirred the development of research questions, theoretical frameworks, and methodologies like no other concept. However, its role as a nexus concept also goes along with a crucial problem. Integrating concepts like life and teleology can easily lead to confusion about what 'organism' actually refers to. This is because, first, these other concepts themselves are quite hard to grasp and, second, they can be weighted and interlaced in many different ways when carving out the unit of the organism. As we will see, this dualism between fruitful versatility, on the one hand, and opacity or fuzziness, on the other, has created opposing positions and alternating phases in the history of

---

[1] For a detailed etymology and history of the terms 'organism,' 'organ,' and 'organization' that considers older traditions since antiquity, see Toepfer (2011).

The organism concept provides an interface for interlinking several other biological and philosophical concepts in different ways. These concepts can be grouped in two clusters: one set informs the organizational dimension of the organism (what internal organization it has), the other set informs its relational dimension (how the organism interacts with its abiotic environment and other organisms). Each dimension may include more related concepts besides the ones depicted in Figure 1. The concept of biological individuality serves as a means to specify this nexus. In other words, different forms of individuality (e.g., physiological or evolutionary individuality) provide us with the 'language' (Figure 1, dotted lines) that allows us to link these associated concepts with that of the organism. For example, if we want to highlight what it means for an organism to be alive, we may describe it is a physiologically or metabolically integrated individual. These different elements of the nexus concept will be spelled out in detail throughout this Element.

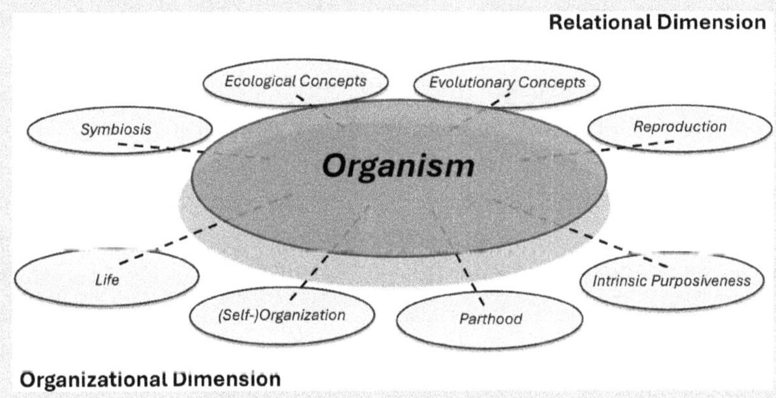

Figure 1 The nexus concept "organism" and its connection to different other biological and philosophical concepts.

biology until today in which organisms have been foregrounded and highlighted or backgrounded and neglected by scientists and philosophers.

2.1 Organized Bodies

Before 'organism' became a widely used term in the early 19th century in biology, in the 17th and 18th century scholars like Locke, Boyle, or Leibniz often spoke of 'organized bodies.' Leibniz, in contrast to Stahl, did not characterize the organisms or organized body as a vital principle. For him the organism rather describes a form in which matter is organized hierarchically and which displays high complexity. The organism is not primarily a purposeful unit of life, as Stahl had suggested, but an organized network of mechanisms (see Echelard-Dumas 1976). While Leibniz still aimed for a science that mechanistically unites the living and non-living, during the 18th century 'mechanism' and 'organism' became increasingly opposing concepts.[2]

The emancipation of 'biology' as a distinct discipline in the 18th century saw rapid experimental developments (Steigerwald 2019). Several of these were linked to new microscopic methodologies. They not only allowed understanding the complex internal differentiation of organisms into various components but made necessary answering the question of how the organism as a whole is constructed and maintained through its mutually related and functionally dependent parts. This view of the organism as a dynamic physiological unit was advanced in contrast to machines and mechanisms. This included characterizing organisms no longer as constituted and ordered through a vital force (Stahl) or even soul (e.g., Gassendi 1658), but based on their internal dynamics and physiological organization. Two important scholars that stirred this development were Leiden-based physiologist and botanist Herman Boerhaave and philosopher Immanuel Kant.

In his influential textbook of physiology *Institutiones medicae*, first published in 1708, as well as in other writings, Boerhaave argues that the "organic body was composed of entirely different parts [. . .] and thus the actions of these parts depend on one another" (Boerhaave 1727, 3). He added that "when they [the parts] are treated they are joined together so that they are a circle as if cause and effect mutually effect each other" (Boerhaave 1708, 11). This idea of organisms as decentrally organized wholes that are built up and physiologically maintained through reciprocally interacting causal parts would be picked up and further developed by Immanuel Kant in his '3rd Critique.'

Kant argued that in 'organized beings' "the parts, with respect to both form and being, are only possible through their relationship to the whole" and "that the parts bind themselves mutually into the unity of a whole in such a way that they are mutually cause and effect of one another" (Kant 1913 [1790/1793], AA 5, 373; see also Lenoir 1982). For Kant, organized beings in nature are self-organizing systems where the unity is achieved through the reciprocal production and maintenance of their parts. Kant closely links this view of the organism as a 'cycle' of physiologically interacting parts with his influential account on teleology. He argues that seemingly purposive features in organisms, like

---

[2] For critiques of mechanistic views of the organism in the 18th century, see Gierer (1996). For a different historiography on the role of mechanistic views in developing the organism concept, see Riskin (2016).

morphological forms apparently designed for certain functions, are in fact a product of this causal reciprocity of parts. Such purposive features, he states, we usually only know from designed objects. He thus claims that, while organisms can be analysed mechanistically as natural objects (i.e., by decomposing them into their single interacting parts), their unity and coherence require a special cognitive ability – teleological reasoning – that views their parts as functional components of a whole and categorizes them as a distinct class of objects.

For example, Kant considered a tree as an organism that self-organizes and maintains its parts (roots, trunk, branches, leaves, etc.) in a way that each part contributes to the tree's overall life and growth. The roots absorb nutrients, the leaves perform photosynthesis, and the branches support the leaves. These parts are not merely mechanically linked but are interdependent, functioning for the purpose of sustaining the whole tree. His proposed solution to study such organized beings is that biologists should draw on teleology as a heuristic tool to temporarily deal with the intricacies of organisms' seemingly purposive features, until mechanistic research catches up and makes us understand their underlying interactions of parts that actually produce these features. In other words, he suggests that biologists should treat organisms 'as if' they show purposiveness, but not assume they actually do (Kant 1913 [1790/1793]; see Desmond and Huneman 2020).

These Kantian ideas – organisms as self-organized and self-maintaining systems of reciprocally interacting parts and teleology as a heuristic to reason about the seemingly purposive coherence of organisms – became engraved in biologists' collective memory. They shaped the way biologists conceptualized organisms, especially during the steadily increasing usage of the organism concept in the mid 19th and early 20th century (see Figure 2).

2.2 Interacting Organisms

In the middle of the 19th century a new dimension of the nexus concept 'organism' emerges: the organism as a *unit of relations*. A unit that is not primarily defined through a look 'inside,' that is, through the organism's internal (self-) organization, but through a look at how it is connected to its outside environment, through ecological interactions with various other organisms and abiotic factors, through reproductive processes, and through selective pressures influencing this unit during evolutionary processes.[3]

---

[3] For a detailed historical and philosophical investigation of the organism–environment relationship, see Fábregas-Tejeda (forthcoming).

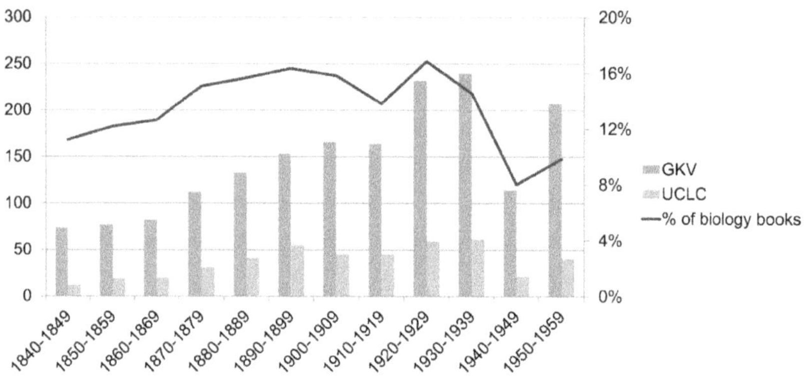

Figure 2 Usage of the organism concept, 1840–1959.
The figure shows the number of monographies carrying in their title 'organism,' 'organisms,' 'Organismus,' or 'Organismen.' Sources are the databases of the British Library (light gray bars) and German Union Catalogue, GVK (dark gray bars). Only biological books are considered. Black graph shows the percentage of all 'organism books' compared with all biological books published per year (i.e., entries in both databases matching keyword or substance for 'biology' or 'Biologie'). Since single books may appear more than one time in each database, multiple counting is possible (see Baedke 2019a, 297).

This new dimension entered the stage, among others, through Charles Darwin (1859), who understands the organism as a body whose changing features over time are the result of its relationship to the environment, through selective pressures acting on it and selecting certain heritable variations rather than others, through reproductive acts between members of a species, and through variation that is in substantial way triggered by the environment.[4] After a phase of lively discussions about the nature of the organism–environment relationship in the late 19th and early 20th century (see Section 4), in the middle of the 20th century, this view of organism–environment interaction was often radicalized toward an understanding of organisms as merely intermediate stages or transition points in a broader evolutionary process in which especially genes and populations, but not organisms, matter (see Section 3). Philosopher Denis Walsh summarizes this view: "[t]he production of whole organisms, and their differential survival and reproduction, are causally necessary consequences of the activities of [genetic] replicators" (Walsh 2017, 243). In the same line, evolution is nothing but a change in gene frequencies within populations. According to this view, championed especially by some

---

[4] Especially the late Darwin, however, also highlighted the idea of the organism as a holistic, functionally organized entity that is not primarily defined by its relationship to its external environment.

population geneticists, organisms were often seen as passive elements adapted to their environment. Their relationship to the environment was asymmetrical and unidirectional (e.g., Williams 1992, 484; see Baedke and Fábregas-Tejeda 2023). This means that evolutionary relevant forces act on organisms; organisms themselves are passive and receptive units, not actively shaping their environment.

In contrast to this view, especially in the early 20th century, several authors conceptualized the organism–environment relationship as a reciprocal and symmetrical one (see Section 4; see also Baedke et al. 2021). For example, inspired by Kant's transcendental philosophy and sensory physiological studies, Jakob von Uexküll (1909, 1928) argued that each organism creates its own environment. He suggested that organisms are intimately connected with their environment, as they subjectively perceive and act within it. The environment consists of a 'perception world' ('Merkwelt'), accessed through sensory receptors and processed neurally, and a complementary 'effect world' ('Wirkwelt'), where the organism interacts causally with the environment through various traits and behaviors, ranging from conditioned reflexes to exploratory actions. Together, the organism's perceptions and actions form a feedback loop, or 'function-circle' ('Funktionskreis'), linking the perceived world and the effect world. During its life the organism passes through a so-called 'environmental tunnel' ('Umwelttunnel', Uexküll 1922) in which the environment and the organism reciprocally act on one another (Figure 3).

Figure 3 Jakob von Uexküll's model of an 'environmental tunnel'.
The organism is depicted as a rolling cogwheel and the environment as its ground. The wheels' joints represent the organism's receptive properties, the pivots represent its action-executing features. Throughout the lifetime of an organism (i.e., the wheel rolls over the underground), it is affected by and affects the environment. Outgoing arrows in the wheel mark the beginning of activities of the organism in the environment; the ingoing arrows mark their ends and the perception of an environmental event (Uexküll 1922, 143; slightly modified).

2.3 The Eclipse of the Organism

In the early 20th century, we see a clear peak in the usage of the concept of the organism (Figure 2). We will return to the various theoretical positions, like organicism as well as neo-Kantianism, holism, and dialectical materialism that tried to establish an organism-centered biology during this time in Section 4. For now, let us focus on the significant decline of the organism concept from the 1940s onward – a development Walsh (2015) has called the 'eclipse of the organism.' This eclipse was characterized by a widespread downgrading of the explanatory roles of the organism in biological research (see Baedke and Fábregas-Tejeda 2023). This included neglecting the value of the mentioned two dimensions of the nexus concept, that is, *the organizational and relational dimensions* of the organism.

First, from the mid 20th century onward new developments in molecular biology and evolutionary biology (which became increasingly gene-centered) dominated the scientific landscape. These fields significantly influenced the explanatory standards of biological research, often downplaying or overlooking the epistemic roles previously attributed to the organism. This included the idea that the organization of organisms and the self-maintenance of their organization is less relevant (the effects of this idea can, e.g., be traced in Figure 2 in the decreasing usage of the organism concept in the 1940–1950s). Instead, the parts of organisms, especially their genes, were attributed stronger causal power. Genes became increasingly disconnected from their organismic context and were viewed as the main determinants of phenotypic traits. As Gawne and colleagues (2018) observed, most evolutionary biologists from the mid 20th century onward adopted a rather simplistic view of the genotype–phenotype map, most often neglecting the need for a comprehensive framework that includes more levels of an organism's organization, rather than just genes. While molecular approaches often pursued a reductionist path that abstracted from the whole organism or described it as a machine (Monod 1971), population geneticists concentrated on allele transmission and dynamics, thus neglecting the developing organism (Walsh 2019). Consequently, the organism's special organization was increasingly sidelined as a central biological problem.

This development in biology was accompanied by a neglect of the issue of organization, and thus of the organism, by philosophy. Prominent philosophers of science at the time, such as Ernest Nagel (1951) and his student Morton Beckner (1959), actively dismissed the importance of organization, considering it irrelevant to biological research (see Brooks forthcoming). Nagel and Beckner rejected vividly the idea, defended by Kant and others, that a study of the organism needs a distinctive mode of investigation and claimed that organization turns out to be a pseudo-problem once biological phenomena were reduced to their underlying chemical and physical processes through mechanistic approaches. This analytical dismissal of the organizational specificity of the organism concept set the stage for a new philosophy of biology starting in the 1960s and 1970s that, for many decades, was primarily interested in genes, molecular biology, and population genetics, rather than in the organism, developmental biology or physiology (see Nicholson and Gawne 2015).[5]

As a second development, the relational dimension of the nexus concept lost its relevance and was significantly narrowed and streamlined. This trend included two components. On the one hand, previous views of organism–environment reciprocity were often replaced by more unidirectional models in which selective pressures of the environment acted on the organism, but not the other way round. Apart from this consideration, any usage of environmental variation and organismal interaction with it could be neglected, as population geneticist Douglas Falconer (1960) argued: For him, the environment is a "source of error" and biologists should "reduce it as much as possible" (140). In this view, the organism loses its previous function as a causal agent that constructs its environment, and thus, due to feedback processes, affects its own development and evolution.

On the other hand, the ideas of agency and teleology were rejected or reformulated. This included various accounts in the second half of the 20th century which argued that one can fully account for organismic purposiveness by citing invariant molecular mechanisms that get transmitted intergenerationally (e.g., Monod 1971; for an analysis, see Walsh 2017). Such a genetic "program is the result of natural selection, constantly adjusted by the selective value of the achieved endpoint" (Mayr 1985 [1974], 141; see also Dobzhansky et al. 1977, 96). In other words, organisms appear as agents merely because genetic programs that encode purposive-like traits were selected over time. This development resulted in the view, widely shared among biologists, that organismal agency was a mere evolutionary *product*, but not a *cause* that has some bearing on developmental or even evolutionary processes.

This development was accompanied by a trend both in science and in philosophy to replace the notions of teleology and purposiveness by that of function. For example, ethologist Konrad Lorenz stated:

> "What does a cat have sharp, curved claws for?" and answer simply "To catch mice with," this does not imply a profession of any *mythical teleology*, but the plain statement that catching mice is the *function* whose survival value, by the process of natural selection, has bred cats with this particular form of claw.

---

[5] For exceptions, see, for example, Wimsatt (1971, 1974).

> Unless selection is at work, the question "What for?" cannot receive an
> answer with any real meaning. (Lorenz 1966, 9; emphasis added)[6]

In sum, these trends led to a scientific and philosophical focus on units like genes, molecular processes, populations, species and concepts like functions and natural selection, rather than on the organism and concepts like organization, the organism–environment relation, teleology, and agency. If discussed at all, biologists and philosophers usually endorsed a much narrower conception of organisms' *organizational dimension* (organisms became primarily the product of genetic programs and there was no need to uncover their special organization) and of their *relational dimension* (organisms were not seen as agents that co-construct their environment and that modulate their developmental and evolutionary trajectories but as passive targets of environmental influences). This development led to the general situation that Brian Goodwin (1999) lamented, when he criticized the disappearance of the organism as a fundamental unit in biology (see Section 1). However, this situation has changed substantially in recent years. Today we see another 'return of the organism' in biology and philosophy of biology.

3 The Return of the Organism in Biology

This section examines the renewed interest in the organism concept in the modern biosciences, particularly in postgenomics and biomedicine as well as in developmental and evolutionary biology. It explores philosophical trends relevant for understanding the organism, like discussions about biological individuality and organismal agency and teleology. Then, two main challenges are identified in line with the organizational and relational traditions of the nexus concept: the 'inward challenge' of understanding the organism's internal organization and individuality and the 'outward challenge' of distinguishing it from its environment, especially when organisms (as agents) deeply interact with their surroundings. Addressing these challenges is key to understanding how organisms impact causal pathways inside of them and in their environment.

3.1 The Organism in Postgenomics and Developmental Evolution

The organism has been rediscovered as a central explanatory unit in biology due to two parallel developments. First, the shift of molecular biology from more gene-centered frameworks toward 'postgenomics' and, second, the renewal of

---

[6] In line with that, philosophy of biology in the late 20th century was more interested in clarifying the concept of function in biology, rather than addressing the long-standing issue of organismal teleology; see, for example, Cummins (1975), Neander (1991).

developmental perspectives on evolution, especially what has been called the 'Extended Evolutionary Synthesis.' Let us discuss these two trends in detail.

Around 2000, the findings of the Human Genome Project uncovered a so-far hidden layer of complexity to biologists' understanding of the relationship between genes and phenotypic traits. Initially, this project was expected to unveil the 'book of life,' as, for example, Richard Dawkins (1976) had characterized the genetic code, and to eliminate all genetic diseases. However, findings revealed in 2001 that the human genome has only about 35,000 genes, far fewer than the anticipated 100,000, and that humans are 99.9 percent identical at the DNA level. Against this background, scientists increasingly realized that genes alone couldn't fully explain the diversity of life or solve global challenges like type-2 diabetes. As a result, the focus of molecular biology shifted to studying how genes function within complex contexts that determine when they are switched on or off. Understanding a gene's expression and influence on a trait now meant considering the broader context, including genomic, cellular, organismic, and environmental factors. The genome was no longer seen as a collection of discrete, stable units but as a complex, dynamic system with countless regulatory components and interactions (Jablonka and Lamb 2014; Baedke 2018).

This insight led to various new research projects in, what some philosophers, social scientists, medical experts, and biologists have called 'postgenomics' (Stotz 2008; Richardson and Stevens 2015; Guttinger and Dupré 2016). Postgenomic research emerged (among others) as a reaction to the Human Genome Project, driven through new developments in fields like epigenetics, proteomics, and exposomics. These studies often adopt a conceptual framework that construes developmental and inheritance processes as open systems characterized by multifactorial dependencies among environmental factors, developmental mechanisms, and the genome (see also Oyama 2000; Moss 2001). It holds that the expression and timing of genetic information are not solely determined by the genes themselves but are heavily influenced by their organismic context and larger environment. This view has influenced new studies of developmental plasticity, robustness, bias, and constraint, accompanied by historical and philosophical investigations of these phenomena (Loison 2024; Nicoglou 2024) and their underlying causal dependencies (Baedke 2018). In addition, it has stimulated new debates on biomedical frameworks and applications.

Postgenomic approaches brought renewed hopes of tackling global health problems, like arthritis, metabolic syndrome, Alzheimer's, mental health, and autism, through interventions that instead of primarily targeting genes, focus on epigenetic regulatory factors, proteins, behavioral patterns, environmental cues, and, more recently, symbiotic microbes. In such approaches to 'environmental health,' the sociocultural, behavioral, and lifestyle patterns (nutrition, hygiene regimes, stress levels, etc.) of humans take center stage (Giroux et al. 2023) or, in more general terms, the organism–environment relation.[7] In addition, new emphasis on the unit of the organism as well as trends in genomics and postgenomics have bolstered developments in so-called 'personalized medicine' and 'precision medicine.' These fields aim to take "into account individual differences in people's genes, environments, and lifestyles" (Sankar and Parker 2017, 743) to develop targeted treatments and preventive measures, to gain a deeper understanding of disease complexity and to tailor therapies to specific patient groups and even individual patients.[8]

Apart from this organismal trend in molecular and developmental biology as well as in biomedicine, we see an accompanying development in *evolutionary biology*. In the past thirty years, new empirical and theoretical approaches in fields such as (ecological) evolutionary developmental biology or (Eco-)Evo-Devo (Minelli 2009; Gilbert and Epel 2015), epigenetics (Jablonka and Lamb 2014, 2020; Müller 2024), niche construction theory (Odling Smee et al. 2003; Laland et al. 2019; Odling-Smee 2024), and microbiome research (Gilbert et al. 2012; Roughgarden et al. 2018; Suárez 2020) have led to a better understanding of how the development and behavior of organisms can bias and drive evolutionary change through their ability to modulate gene activity, their plasticity, and capacity to construct their own niche. Here are some examples of recent findings from these fields stirring organismal perspectives on evolution:

(1) *Studies in (Eco-)Evo-Devo* uncover the genetics mechanisms and biochemical pathways underlying the development and evolution of morphological forms (see Minelli 2009; Gilbert and Epel 2015). These studies offer insight into, for example, the evolution of body segments in fruit flies and the eyespot patterns in butterfly wings (see Figure 4), as well as fin-to-limb transitions or digit evolution and loss in tetrapods. They clarify both the plasticity and stability of traits in evolution (e.g., through developmental bias and constraint) and the likeliness of particular variations to occur.

(2) *Studies on environmentally sensitive, extra-genetic information transfer* address how such transmission produces selectable variation which links

---

[7] This development has also led to a new renaissance of the environment concept in biomedical research (Baedke and Buklijas 2023). Unfortunately, it did not allow overcoming older views of genetic determinism. Instead, these views were rather replaced by new forms of postgenomic and environmental determinisms (Baedke et al. 2023–2025; Merlin and Giroux 2024). We will return to this problem in Section 5.

[8] At the moment, however, there remain several uncertainties about the biological significance and diagnostic value these fields provide for individual patients. For a critical discussion, see Lohse (2023).

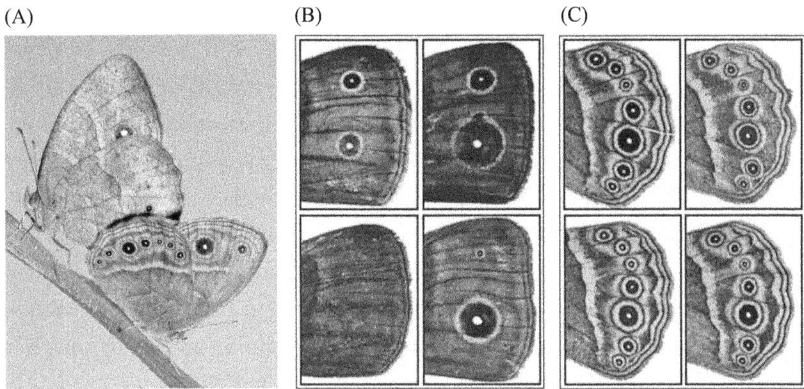

Figure 4 Development and evolution of butterfly eyespots in *Bicyclus anynana*. Eyespots in butterflies can confuse predators, and can vary in size and color. Allen et al. (2008) have tested how far these variations could evolve by artificially selecting for different eyespot traits in *Bicyclus anynana* (A). They successfully produced butterflies with quite different sizes of each eyespots (B). Here, variation could be produced seemingly without restriction in the population. However, they could not achieve the same flexibility with the color composition (C). For example, one cannot produce one eyespot with a big black ring and another with a thinner black ring. This suggests that while size is easy to modify, color is constrained by developmental mechanisms. The study highlights that for understanding how variation is produced in evolution and why certain evolutionary trajectories are more likely than others, constraints in organisms' developmental processes, from gene-expression patterns to cell and tissue interactions, need to be investigated. (A: Photograph by William Piel and Antónia Monteiro (CC BY 4.0), B and C: Photographs reproduced with permission of BioMed Central Ltd. (Allen et al. 2008)).

development and evolution (Jablonka and Lamb 2020). This includes a large number of heritable regulatory factors (from DNA methylations, histone modifications, and noncoding RNAs) and different modes of non-genetic transmissions, including somatic and parental effects (e.g., maternal factors being transferred via the placenta and lactation or traits that are behaviorally induced through parent–offspring interactions) as well as transgenerational and germ line-mediated inheritance (e.g., inheritance of pathogen resistance in *Arabidopsis thaliana* for nine generations, transmission of obesity in *Mus musculus* for six generations, and inheritance of eye color in *Drosophila melanogaster* for more than fifty generations; see Fitz-James and Cavalli 2022).

(3) *Studies in microbiome research* show that symbiotic microbes are major environmental agents influencing development and possibly evolution (Gilbert et al. 2012). Microbes contribute to normal development: for example, specific bacteria acquired at birth are essential for developing the immune system and gut capillaries in mice by inducing gene expression in host cells. Microbial metabolites from the mother's diet also aid fetal development, including brain and pancreas maturation, and microbes obtained during birth are crucial for intestinal, immune, and neural development (Kimura et al. 2020). Studies also suggest that changes in symbionts could provide selectable variants for evolution and could open new evolutionary trajectories (Zhang et al. 2019; Gilbert 2020).

(4) *Studies in niche construction theory* show how organisms' behaviors can influence the niche that surrounds them and thus modulate the selective pressures affecting them and other species (Odling-Smee et al. 2003). Examples include animals building artifacts such as nests, burrows, and mounds, and plants creating shade and altering nutrient cycling. Clark and colleagues (2020) demonstrated that niche construction can influence the variability and intensity of natural selection, allowing for a distinction between constructed and non-constructed environmental sources of selection.[9]

The processes summarized above can cooccur and create complex webs of interrelated developmental, symbiotic, and evolutionary processes that are difficult to disentangle. For an example of such a process, see Box 2.[10]

Building on these findings, biologists and philosophers of biology have defended developmentally oriented approaches to evolution that called for

---

Box 2 Niche construction effects adaptation of red flour beetle (*Tribolium castaneum*) to bacterium.

Lai Ka Lo and colleagues (2025) studied how niche construction can aid adaptation in group-living animals by improving their match with the environment. They conducted an experimental evolution study with red flour beetles (*Tribolium castaneum.* Figure 5A: adult) and their natural parasite *Bacillus thuringiensis tenebrionis* (Btt). Btt forms spores that infect beetle larvae (Figure 5B) via the oral route, disrupting the function

---

[9] For an overview of these four developments and more detailed discussions of relevant empirical findings, see Jablonka and Lamb (2020), Baedke and Gilbert (2024), and Lala et al. (2024).

[10] This study was conducted in the lab of Joachim Kurtz, University Münster. To my knowledge it is the first experimental proof of how niche construction leads to new adaptive traits across generations.

Box 2 (cont.)

of their digestive track, which eventually leads to the death of the host. Adult beetles modify their environment through quinone-rich stink gland secretions that alter the surrounding microflora, including that of Btt. In other words, beetles co-construct their local (bacterial) niche. In this study a specific gene (via RNAi) was knocked down to impede the production of stink gland secretions, which allowed exposing beetles to different constructed niches (flour conditioning by stink gland secreting beetles or no constructed environment in knockdown beetles). After three generations of experimental selection for resistance to Btt, beetle populations with functional niche construction (with secretion) showed the strongest survival increase against Btt infection. After nine generations, beetles evolving with imparied niche construction caught up, and they developed faster and produced slightly more offspring, suggesting potential costs of niche construction. Intriguingly, studying the genetic underpinnings of the evolved resistance using a whole-genome transcriptomic analysis uncovered that beetles evolving with impaired niche construction had achieved resistance to Btt in different ways than beetles evolving with niche construction. This study shows how microbiota interaction of organisms and their niche construction can have various feedback effects on their development, reproduction, and evolution of adaptive traits. In addition, since *Bacillus thuringiensis* is used commercially as biopesticide to control insects in agricultural and public health context, these evolutionary effects on beetles' immunity may have a larger societal relevance.

Figure 5 Flour beetles *Tribolium castaneum*, adult (A) and larvae (B). (Photos reproduced from Kahn et al. 2016, with permission of John Wiley and Sons.)

broadening evolutionary theory (West-Eberhard 2003; Pigliucci and Müller 2010; Jablonka and Lamb 2014, 2020; Laland et al. 2014, 2015; Müller 2017; Edelaar et al. 2023; Lala et al. 2024; see Huneman and Walsh 2017; Fábregas-Tejeda and Vergara-Silva 2018; Baedke et al. 2020a). They propose that evolutionary change should be examined mainly within developing and interacting organisms. They suggest rejecting orthodox views, prevalent especially in population genetics, which claim that "allele frequency change [in populations] caused by natural selection is the only credible process underlying the evolution of adaptive organismal traits" (Charlesworth et al. 2017). Instead, they argue that organisms' responses to environmental cues and phenotypic variation can create nonrandom changes – like environmentally induced changes in regulatory processes and physical constraints during development – that can influence evolution. In line with this view, West-Eberhard (2003, 2005), proposed that genes often follow rather than lead in evolution and that, in fact, organisms introduce new phenotypes that genes then stabilize later.

Against this background, evolutionary biologist Kevin Lala and colleagues (Laland et al. 2014, 161) suggest that "an alternative vision of evolution is beginning to crystallize." This new "organism-centered perspective" (Laland et al. 2015) stresses the idea that organisms are the central explanatory units to understand evolutionary relevant dynamics in (gene-)regulatory processes during embryo- and morphogenesis, the origin of heritable variation, and shifts in selective pressures of niches. This new framework has been labeled the 'Extended Evolutionary Synthesis.' Denis Walsh describes it as follows:

> The evolutionary biology of our own century suggests that the exclusive reliance on the dynamics of populations ushered in by the Modern Synthesis must be augmented, or perhaps even replaced, by an account of the ways that *organisms* participate in and direct the process of evolution. (Walsh 2021, 281; emphasis added)

Such calls for an *organism-centered view of evolution* are not new, however. Previously evolutionary biologist Stephen J. Gould (1980, 129) argued that a reformed theory of evolution should reintroduce "to biology a concept of organism" and philosopher Susan Oyama (2000, 31) suggested to 'restore the organism' in evolutionary research.

These two developments – one in postgenomics and one in evolutionary biology – have led to a 'return of the organism' (Huneman 2010; Nicholson 2014; Baedke 2019a) in biology. These trends were accompanied and supported by developments in philosophy of biology that focused on organismal topics and issues around biological individuality and agency.

3.2 Organisms as Individuals and Agents

In the past twenty years, philosophy of biology expanded its scope from focusing mainly on issues like the concept of the gene or the nature of selection toward also including topics that operate on the level of organisms. This development, first, includes an intensive discussion of what the unit of a *biological individual* is. To what entity do biologists refer to when they speak of 'individuals'? In recent years, philosophers have explored various conceptual frameworks of biological individuality, from evolutionary individuality (a coherent unit that evolves or is selected; e.g., Hull 1980; Godfrey-Smith 2013) and ecological individuality (an integrated unit of ecological interactions; e.g., Huneman 2021) to developmental, physiological, or immunological individuality (e.g., metabolically closed units or entities that draw boundaries around them based on their immune reactions to environmental factors; e.g., Dupré and O'Malley 2009; Pradeu 2010). Other issues concern questions about boundaries between individuals and collectives (e.g., between hosts and their microbes or individual bees and their colony), how new levels of individuality develop and evolve (e.g., multicellular units), how the complex plurality of different criteria to individuate biological units in nature relate to one another, and what role they play for different research practices and disciplines.[11]

When philosophers or biologists speak of 'individuals,' in fact, what they often mean is 'organisms.' From an historical perspective this is not surprising, as the two concepts have a shared history. In fact, since the end of the 18th century, both concepts were increasingly used interchangeably (Cheung 2006). Even today, no consensus has been reached on whether organismality and individuality are interchangeable or distinct concepts. For example, philosopher Elselijn Kingma (2020, 1037) says: "What is the problem of biological individuality? Organisms are amongst the central entities with which the biological sciences are concerned [. . .]. I use the terms 'biological individual' and 'organism' interchangeably." Similar views are adopted by several authors (see, e.g., Gardner and Grafen 2009; Folse and Roughgarden 2010; Clarke 2011, 2013).

Guido Prieto (2023) argues that despite the wide interest in the concept of biological individuality, so far, philosophers of biology have ignored addressing this problem. This has the consequence that both concepts "are so inextricably comingled that they could hardly be spelled out independently from one another" (47). He warns that instead of blurring the difference between the

---

[11] For an overview of these debates and different position of biological individuality, see for example, Bouchard and Huneman (2013), Pradeu (2016), Lidgard and Nyhart (2017), Baedke (2019b), Kaiser and Trappes (2021), McConwell (2023).

two, scholars should identify possible criteria for demarcating them.[12] One solution adopted by some biologists and philosophers is to interpret organisms as a special kind of individual. Often, following the historically influential view of 'organized bodies' by Boerhaave, Kant and others, they understand the organism as a self-organized physiological individual (e.g., Pradeu 2016). Yet others speak of organisms as units of ecological interaction or selection.

I suggest that we can understand the relationship between biological individuality and organismality by drawing on the idea of the 'nexus concept' (see Section 2; Box 1). If we understand 'organism' as forming the nexus in a web of interrelated concepts that can be grouped into an *organizational dimension* (concepts like life or self-organization) and a *relational dimension* (with reproductive, ecological, and evolutionary concepts), then the different forms of biological individuality may serve as a means to specify and harden this nexus. In other words, they are the 'language' or 'mediator' that allows us to link these associated concepts with that of the organism. If we want to highlight in a specific philosophical or empirical context what it means for an organism to be alive or to have a self-organized structure, we may say it is a physiological or metabolic individual. If we want to highlight what it means for an organism to interact with other entities in its environment or that it is a target of selection, we may say it is a reproductive, ecological, or evolutionary individual. In short, individuality provides us with the knots that link organismality with organizational and relational concepts. It is crucial to create the nexus.[13]

This process of knotting together concepts is not without problems. Some views of individuality and thus some organizational and relational perspectives of the organism cannot be fully integrated. This becomes especially relevant when studying the phenomena of developmental evolution discussed in the last section. If we consider individual organisms as the primary entities partaking both in development and evolution, any effort to integrate these domains must prove that it is, in fact, the same unit that develops and evolves. This is where the problem occurs. Evolutionary individuals are typically seen as reproductive units with differential fitness and shared lineages (so-called 'Darwinian individuals'; Godfrey-Smith 2013) or as units of selection (so-called 'interactors';

---

[12] Prieto (2023) goes on and systematizes different ways how biological individuality and organismality have been coupled in the literature and which conceptual challenges these different accounts face when trying to disentangle the two (see also Prieto 2024).

[13] This view allows that biological individuality may serve other roles in biology, not linked to organisms, like individuating supra- and super-organismal entities. For example, evolutionary individuality could be ascribed to entities like genes or populations. In addition, it does not presuppose that both the organizational and relational dimensions of the 'organism nexus' can be unified by a shared concept like 'organizational closure' (see Moreno and Mossio 2015). In fact, with the help of 'individuality' both dimensions can only be integrated in the organism concept to a certain degree.

Hull 1980). However, these categories do not always align with criteria of physiological individuality (Godfrey-Smith 2013; Pradeu 2016). For example, some host-microbiota systems form a highly integrated physiological and immunological individual. In fact, humans and their gut microbiota form together a metabolically and immunologically closed unit that jointly coordinates internal processes and interactions with the environment. But these systems often do not constitute a unified reproductive or evolutionary unit with a shared lineage (e.g., humans' genes and their microbes are transmitted independently). Therefore, views of organisms understood as physiological individuals and organisms understood as evolutionary individuals are not always compatible. This means that there are limitations for integrating different views of individuality and thus of linking particular organizational and relational perspectives of the organism. In short, the organism is a nexus of conceptual integrations, but also of conceptual tensions.

There is a second debate about the organism that recently shaped the philosophical landscape – that of *organismal agency* and *teleology*. While these topics have been long-debated in the history of philosophy and biology, especially in the early 20th century with a diversity of holistic, organicist, and neo-Kantian positions (see Baedke 2024; Fábregas-Tejeda 2024), during the second half of the 20th century these discussions vanished most widely. In fact, substantial attempts were made to limit agential and teleological reasoning to studies of developmental processes that differed from non-teleological evolutionary processes (Mayr 1961) or to treat purposiveness not as an intrinsic feature of organisms but as a product of natural selection (i.e., so-called 'teleonomy,' Pittendrigh 1958; see Dresow and Love 2023). These frameworks usually attributed organismal agency to 'external teleology' (purposefulness as a result of external selective forces) rather than 'internal teleology' or 'intrinsic purposiveness,' which was dismissed as vitalism (Baedke and Fábregas-Tejeda 2023). As a result, discussions on evolved, purposeful organismic agency were limited during this time (but see, e.g., Russell 1950; Piaget 1976).

However, this situation has clearly changed in recent years. Today, interest in organismal agency has reemerged (e.g., Toepfer 2012; Moreno and Mossio 2015; Walsh 2015; Riskin 2016; Okasha 2018; Rupik 2024; Fábregas-Tejeda et al. 2024). New developmentalist perspectives, such as niche construction theory and plasticity-led evolution, have shifted away from viewing agency solely as a product of adaptation and reopened debates on 'internal teleology' (Walsh 2021; Sultan et al. 2022; Jaeger 2024). These discussions reconsider the role of agency and teleology in development and evolution, asking whether adopting the position of internal teleology can enhance our understanding of these processes and how biologists should conceptualize organisms' apparent purposiveness – through concepts like goal-directedness, self-organization, autonomy and control, or by drawing on the idea of 'affordances' (Moreno and Mossio 2015; Walsh 2015; Babcock and McShea 2024).[14] Further questions arise regarding whether agency is limited to goal-directed behaviors and environmental interactions or can also be attributed to (all or only certain) developmental processes, such as plasticity (Sultan et al. 2022; Nahas 2024; Walsh and Sultan 2024). Additionally, what evolutionary consequences stem from organisms' agential activities, like in the case of the red flour beetle (Box 2), in contrast to non-agential activities?

This ongoing debate presents a range of positions. On one side we find ontological views, which argue that agency and purposiveness in developmental evolution are intrinsic capacities of organisms (see Nahas and Sachs 2023). On the other side, there are classical Kantian perspectives, which see agency as merely an epistemic tool for biologists to navigate the complexities of development and evolution (see Desmond and Huneman 2020). Some of the latter views tie in with a tradition of neo-Kantian authors which highlighted in the late 19th and early 20th century that teleology is the condition for the availability of organisms as biological objects of investigation (see Toepfer 2024). Heinrich Rickert expressed this idea as follows:

> [T]his science [i.e. biology] can be defined in such a way that it deals with bodies whose parts unite to form a teleological unity, indeed, this concept of unity is so inseparable from the concept of organism that we call living beings 'organisms' only because of the teleological unity [. . .]. A science of organisms without any teleological moment would be a *contradictio in adjecto*. (Rickert 1902, 456; German original; emphasis in original; see Toepfer 2024).

This position suggests that teleology is a method or way of thought that enables us to access a specific class of objects – organisms. This class could not be studied by mechanistic accounts alone.

These two recent philosophical debates about biological individuality and agency will hopefully provide new clarifications of the *unity* and *activity* that is unique to organisms in contrast to other biological entities. Before we return to these issues in Section 4, let us focus on two long-standing central conceptual challenges that the nexus concept of the organism faces. Answering them will be crucial for developing an organism-centered biology.

---

[14] The concept of affordance refers to what an organism can do based on its traits and its environment together. Walsh (2015) argues that organisms are not passive objects of evolutionary forces, but active agents that co-create the affordances shaping evolution. As organisms pursue their goals and navigate their 'affordance landscapes,' they actively participate in constructing the conditions of their existence, thereby enacting evolution.

3.3 Two Conceptual Challenges

The above trends in biology and philosophy of biology clearly point toward a return of the organism concept in 21st century biology. This new organism-centered biology usually defends (at least one of) two theoretical and methodological cornerstones:

> Cornerstone 1: *Contextualizing genes and cells in development*:
> Biologists should highlight cellular, organismal, and developmental contexts of gene activity and cellular differentiation, and study the impact of these contextual wholes in shaping developmental and evolutionary processes. Evolutionary biologists should not abstract from these organismal contexts when measuring changes in gene activities and frequencies.

> Cornerstone 2: *Recognizing organisms' actions in their environment*:
> Biologists should understand development and evolution as the result of organism–environment reciprocal interaction. Organisms co-construct their environment, and environmental construction feeds back on organisms. Evolutionary biologists should not understand this relationship in a unidirectional way, in which external environmental factors merely cause changes on genes frequencies and thus population dynamics.

In short, these cornerstones suggest that the organism is considered the central causal unit that modulates inwardly the activity of genes in development, and outwardly its environment and thus its own selection pressures. In recent empirical research, the first cornerstone is usually defended in postgenomics, Evo-Devo and research on developmental plasticity; the second one usually in niche construction theory and Eco-Evo-Devo and studies on behaviorally mediated extra-genetic inheritance. Biologist Richard Lewontin once summarized the second cornerstone as follows:

> Organisms within their individual lifetimes and in the course of their evolution as a species do not adapt to environments; they construct them. They are not simply objects of the laws of nature, altering themselves to bend to the inevitable, but active subjects transforming nature according to its laws. (Lewontin 1982, 163).

In evolutionary biology, the two cornerstones imply seeing organisms not merely as end points of adaptive processes, but as causal starting points of evolutionary trajectories. They can bias or drive evolution by controlling the availability of variation (inwardly) and modulating selection pressures (outwardly). This view is often thought to complement the 'survival of the fittest' perspective of the standard evolutionary theory by an organismal one that better explains the 'arrival of the fittest' (Wagner 2014), that is, how variation emerges that then, later, is selected.

Let me highlight two central conceptual challenges that this new organism-centered biology faces based on these cornerstones. I call them the 'Inward Challenge' and 'Outward Challenge'. They concern the following questions:

Inward Challenge:	What is the internal organization of the organism that constitutes its individuality in contrast to other units in nature?
Outward Challenge:	How can we grasp the organism–environment relationship and separate the organism from its environment, even though both are deeply and reciprocally intertwined?

These challenges correspond to the *organizational dimension* of the nexus concept of the organism and its *relational dimension*. I hold that these two challenges need to be addressed by any version of organism-centered biology in order to clarify how organisms in unique ways (compared to other units of life) affect causal pathways inside and outside of them in development, physiology, ecology, and evolution.

In the next section, we will trace the history of addressing these challenges in past and present attempts to establish an organism-centered biology. We will identify shortcoming and limitations of these approaches and develop new solutions for both challenges.

4 Organism-Centered Biology in the Early 20th Century and Today

Despite the touch of novelty that envelops current organismal trends in biology and philosophy, the idea to found biology on the concept of the organism (instead of other units, like genes, cells, communities, populations, or species) is anything but new. It has been a central idea especially in early 20th century theoretical biology and philosophy of biology, particularly within intellectual movements like organicism, neo-Kantianism, holistic biology, and dialectical materialism. This section starts from the assumption that we can learn to avoid pitfalls of conceptualizing organisms and theorizing about them in today's biology by studying similar past approaches. Therefore, first, I provide an introduction to biophilosophical debates in the early 20th century and their efforts to base biology on the organism biology. Then, I explore how these approaches tackled both the 'inward' and 'outward' challenges and what theoretical solutions they proposed. I will argue that their solutions had significant limitations. Unfortunately, these older positions together with their shortcomings, resurface in the contemporary 'return of the organism.' They result in inconsistent positions that defend both individualistic and anti-individualistic perspectives on the organism. In other words, they highlight the organism, but at the same time lose track of it or dissolve it in its environment. To address these issues, I propose a new conceptual framework that not only defines organisms and their boundaries more clearly, but also emphasizes their essential role as active, creative agents in developmental evolution.

4.1 No Vitalism, No Mechanism, but Organicism and Holism

Before the organism concept came under attack by molecular and evolutionary biologists and by analytical philosophers in the second half of the 20th century, in the first decades of the century and especially in the interwar period, this situation was the exact opposite.[15] While the organism concept also played important roles in romantic 'Naturphilosophie' and in the early days of institutionalizing biology in the late 18th and early 19th centuries (see Köchy 1997; Steigerwald 2019; Rupik 2024), it is in the first half of the 20th century that the organism category took an unprecedented and, so far, unparalleled position in biological theory.

During this time, heated debates over the conceptual, epistemological, and ontological foundations of biology emerged in philosophy and the new field of theoretical biology. These discussions centered on three main issues (see also Laubichler 2017; Baedke 2019a; Baedke et al. 2024a, 2024b):

(1) Biologists and philosophers were worried about a gap between a rapidly growing body of new empirical data and the absence of comprehensive theoretical frameworks, resulting in a 'data crisis' around 1900. The introduction of new experimental techniques led to the collection of data especially about organisms' development, such as plasticity, regeneration, morphogenesis, and about inheritance (Driesch 1892; Morgan 1910; Spemann and Mangold 1924; see Baedke and Brandt 2022). However, much of this new information proved challenging to interpret.

(2) Another part of these debates concerned problems of how to establish a conceptual foundation for biology based on these new findings. For example, these results caused scientists to question basic assumptions, especially regarding the relationship between development and evolution. More generally, scholars became increasingly critical of whether biology's growing specialization of empirical approaches in various new disciplines would not also lead to a theoretical and conceptual fragmentation of biology (see Harwood 1993).

---

[15] For a detailed version of the following historical analysis, see Baedke and Fábregas-Tejeda (2023).

(3) As a consequence, they felt that more thorough philosophical reflections of the epistemological and methodological foundations of biological research were necessary. Scholars increasingly felt that the dominant philosophical frameworks – vitalism and mechanism – that had long shaped their research were limited. They argued that both approaches were proving inadequate for organizing their new findings (Nicholson and Gawne 2015). Mechanism tended to overlook the unique, irreducible, and goal-directed teleological aspects of organisms, trying to reduce them to purely physical processes. In contrast, vitalism (at least in its metaphysical form) directly addressed these phenomena but clashed with the materialist foundation necessary for a scientific explanation of biological processes.

Zoologist Julius Schaxel (1919) summarized this problematic situation by stating that biology is in a 'state of crisis.' In fact, he argued that biology "constitutes of a collection of disorganized, nonequivalent theories, of which many are not even worthy of the name" (Schaxel 1919, 4; German original).[16]

In order to face this 'crisis,' various biologists and philosophers started to reexamine fundamental concepts, especially that of the organism. In the following decades, several approaches emerged which argued that the organism is (one of) the most central theoretical concepts in biology and that biology should be rebuilt based on it – first in German-speaking countries, then in Great Britain and the United States (Haraway 2004 [1976]; Nicholson and Gawne 2014, 2015; Esposito 2016; Peterson 2016; Baedke 2019a; Baedke et al. 2024a). This new organism-centered biology had many different philosophical foundations: neo-Kantianism (e.g., Eduard von Hartmann, Otto Liebmann), holism (including German 'Ganzheitsbiologie'; e.g., Adolf Meyer-Abich, Emil Ungerer, Kurt Goldstein), dialectical materialism (e.g., Julius Schaxel, John Desmond Bernal), and organicism (e.g., Ludwig von Bertalanffy, Joseph Henry Woodger, and Conrad Hal Waddington).[17] For these scholars, 'organism' served as a 'proto-concept' in biology (Bertalanffy 1928, 74) and biologists were asked to adopt an 'organismic understanding of biology' (Schaxel 1919, 125); a position labeled 'organicism' by John Scott Haldane (1917, 3) and 'organismalism' by William Emerson Ritter (1919, I 28).

---

[16] There are interesting similarities of the situation in the early 20th century with today's big data-driven research in the biosciences (e.g., in genomics and metagenomics) and the worrying lack of theory in the field (e.g., Nakagawa et al. 2025).

[17] Exploring these theories about the organism also sheds light on the early development of philosophy of biology. Contrary to the common view that the field emerged in the 1960–1970s, with a primary focus on gene-related issues, its roots lie in early 20th-century debates centered on the organism. These discussions at the intersection of philosophy and theoretical biology played a key role in shaping the philosophy of biology (Nicholson and Gawne 2015; Baedke et al. 2024a, 2024b; Toepfer 2024).

Despite some differences between these approaches, members of this organismic movement shared two core beliefs (Nicholson and Gawne 2015). First, they agreed that the organism is the central ontological unit in biology. It transcends the properties of its individual parts, such as genes or cells, and influences their organization in conjunction with environmental factors. The organism also actively shapes its environment. Second, they maintained that the organism should serve as the fundamental basis for scientific explanations in various biological subfields. This means that studying the organization of the organism is key to understanding biological processes. This includes evolutionary processes, where the organism must be considered the primary unit of analysis, too.

These accounts integrated aspects of both mechanism and vitalism and broke with the traditional divide between the two schools (Allen 2005). They tried to open up a 'third way' that offers an understanding of organisms' unique features (e.g., their intrinsic purposiveness and goal-directed behavior, their self-organization, or robustness despite environmental change) while avoiding both the reductionism of mechanistic approaches and the mystical explanations of metaphysical forms of vitalism. This framework posited that biology requires a focus on the relation between the organism as a whole and the organization of its parts as well as those between organisms and their environment.

This organism-centered biology – while largely forgotten today – laid the conceptual and theoretical groundwork for future organismal discussions in biology, including that for the current return of the organism (see Baedke and Fábregas-Tejeda 2023).[18] In fact, it shares the basic two cornerstones (see Section 3.3) with its contemporary twin. First, it highlighted the organism's unique role affecting causal pathways in development, by modulating and controlling the organization of its parts (be it genes, cells, or organs). For example, Edward Stuart Russell (1930, 240, fn1) claimed that "[t]he parts are the way in which the whole [organism] organizes itself." Others argued that the organism as a whole precedes the parts temporally or even ontologically. Thus, the organism as a whole must be the primary focus in studying changes in organization and development.

Second, this older organism-centered biology also shares the second cornerstone with current approaches, as they highlighted organisms' actions in their environment and the reciprocity of organism–environment relations (see Baedke et al. 2021; Fábregas-Tejeda forthcoming). Various authors developed proto-niche construction frameworks (e.g., Whitehead 1925, 163) and ideas of reciprocity. John Scott Haldane (1884, 32–33) argued: "The organism is thus no more determined by the surrounding than it at the same time determines them.

---

[18] These ideas traveled along complicated historical pathways until today. For example, they served as the theoretical background of Levins and Lewontin's (1985) influential book, however the authors did not acknowledge this older and rich theoretical tradition they drew on.

The two stand to one another, not in the relation of cause and effect, but in that of reciprocity." Others, like Jakob von Uexküll described a reciprocal 'function circle' between the inside and outside of organisms (see Section 2) and Conrad H. Waddington argued that since animals modulate their selection pressures though habitat choice "[n]atural selection is far from being as external a force as the conventional picture might lead one at first sight to believe" (Waddington 1959, 1635–1636). He concluded that "[w]e have to think in terms of circular and not merely unidirectional causal sequences" (Waddington 1960, 400) when reasoning about organisms' relations to their environment.

The past and present versions of an organism-centered biology do not only share an emphasis on the special role the organism plays in affecting causal pathways inside of them and in their environment. Both versions of organism-centered biology also face the same two challenges – the *inward challenge* to conceptually clarify the organism's unique internal organization, and the *outward challenge* to separate organisms from their environment while being inextricably linked with it. Unfortunately, as I will show now, both developed insufficient solutions for these challenges.

4.2 Losing the Organism

If we have a closer look at the theoretical solutions for the 'inward' and 'outward' challenges provided by early 20th century organism-centered biology, we come to see that, though promising, they have significant shortcomings. Most crucially, they lead to views of the organism that, in fact, lose track of its unique characteristics or tend to dissolve it into its environment. In other words, while these accounts aim to highlight the organism, they often lose it instead. Unfortunately, this inconsistency between defending both individualistic and anti-individualistic perspectives on the organism resurfaces in the contemporary 'return of the organism.' To develop this argument in detail let us have a closer look at how past and present account address the above two challenges.

Inward Challenge: Persistence Ain't Enough

To solve the inward challenge means identifying a characteristic intrinsic pattern of organization that is *organismal* in kind, that is, it is not shared by other living beings or units in nature.[19] One traditionally influential view for large parts of past and present organism-centered biology and philosophy of biology draws on conceptualizations of organisms as individual living systems with functional differentiation of parts and a reciprocal interaction of these

---

[19] For a different answer to this inward challenge, compared to the one given in this Element, see Prieto (2024).

parts, which creates and maintains organisms as integrated wholes. This tradition was introduced in the end of the 18th century, when the concepts of organism and life-form were increasingly used interchangeably (i.e., organisms are paradigmatic living beings with a particular organization). It follows the footsteps of scholars like Boerhaave, Kant, and many others and their understanding of 'organized body.' A reoccurring theme in this account is that organisms are individual living bodies that show *self-organization* and *self-maintenance*. As such, the organism is a functionally integrated whole that coordinates their interacting parts so that it *persists* as a whole through time. This understanding of organisms has taken many different forms over the years:

➤ Metabolic or immunological views (e.g., organisms are metabolically self-organized open systems; Haldane 1917; Woodger 1929).
➤ Thermodynamic views (i.e., organisms are autonomous systems that maintain themselves far from thermodynamic equilibrium; Bertalanffy 1942, Schrödinger 1944).
➤ Views of autopoiesis (i.e., organisms are living systems with a circular and recursive biochemical structure that allows producing and sustaining their parts and thus maintaining the whole system; Maturana and Varela 1980 [1972]) and related views of organizational closure and biological autonomy (i.e., organisms are self-regulating and self-determining living beings whose operations and internal constraints mutually depend on one another, thus determining the conditions of existence of the organism; Mossio and Moreno 2010; Moreno and Mossio 2015).[20]

Many of these views are inspired by examples of physiology and phenomena of physiologically self-regulating and -maintaining living systems. They usually characterize organisms as functionally, metabolically, and thermodynamically organized physiological units. For example, Pradeu (2016) states: "It is historically much more accurate to use the word 'organism' to refer to a physiological individual than to an evolutionary individual." Along similar lines, early proponents of an organism-centered biology like Ludwig von Bertalanffy argued that the "living organism [...] remains or establishes its state, by means of constant change of those substances and energies that build up the system as well as during external perturbations" (Bertalanffy 1932, 86). He went on to calculate the maintenance costs for the metabolic unit of the organism given different food

---

[20] On the terminology of the latter approach: 'Constraints' are understood as entities (e.g., enzymes, DNA) that control biological dynamics (processes, reactions, etc.), for example, in chemical reactions during the digestion of food in the gut. 'Closure of constraints' happens when parts of organisms act as constraints on each other, and they realize a mutual dependence, thus stabilizing and maintaining the whole organization of the organism.

availability and how this affects its growth rate. Contemporary representatives of this tradition, like Mossio and Moreno (2010, 270), define the organism as unit with a "particularly complex kind of self-maintenance."

In line with this influential physiological focus on organisms' self-maintenance as living system, philosophers have recently characterized organisms as 'persisters': Peter Godfrey-Smith (2013, 25) argues: "Organisms are essentially persisters, systems that use energy to resist the forces of decay, and only contingently things that reproduce." Following this idea, Subrena E. Smith contends:

> *Persistence*, in this sense, is an ontogenetic rather than a phylogenetic notion. It pertains to individual organisms' spatiotemporal careers. [. . .] Organisms, in order to persist, must have well-differentiated and well-integrated phenotypes that enable them to respond to the contingencies that they encounter. The integration of differentiated parts, which allows for phenotypic accommodation, provides the basis for the idea that organisms are in some sense whole systems [. . .]. (Smith 2017; emphasis added)

While this influential tradition surely allows grasping some important organizational characteristic of organisms, one might wonder whether this characterization is precise enough to single out organisms.[21] How do we distinguish the self-maintained organization of organisms from that of other living beings, as this characterization is also applicable to other functionally integrated, internally differentiated, self-organizing units (wholes) on different levels of organization? In fact, a number of authors have endorsed, for example, the framework of organizational closure to conceptualize symbiotic relations between different organisms (Bich 2019), ecosystems (Nunes-Neto et al. 2014; El-Hani et al. 2024), and eusocial insect colonies (Canciani et al. 2019).[22] In a similar manner, Smith (2017) applies her criteria of persistence on other units in nature, that do not intuitively qualify as organisms. This includes siphonophorae (e.g., the colonial entity Portuguese man o' war), a beehive, and holobionts (i.e., highly integrated symbiotic systems consisting of a host and many taxa of microbiota living in and on the host; Gilbert et al. 2012; Baedke et al. 2020b). Smith argues that one may rightfully say

---

[21] On this problem see also Prieto (2023, 2024), who highlights the lack of precision in past and present accounts when distinguishing the concepts of organism and living being.

[22] Possibly because of such wider applications of the framework, more recently, Mossio (2024, 2) highlighted that at least organization alone is not enough to identify organisms: "Let me point out right away that organization is typically, but not exclusively realized by organisms. For instance, it might be argued that colonies, symbioses, or, at a higher level of description, ecosystems can be described as organized systems, although they would not necessarily count as organisms. Accordingly, the notion of 'organization' and that of 'organism' should not be straightforwardly conflated, although they are closely related: organisms are organized systems, but organized systems are not necessarily organisms."

that all these systems are persisters, with parts maintaining a larger functional whole: zooids' interactions maintain a Portuguese man o' war, individual bees maintain the survival of the beehive, and gut bacteria physiologically and immunologically maintain the symbiotic unit with a multicellular host like *Homo sapiens*.

The fear here is that this approach leads to an inflationary understanding of organismality – a shortcoming from which also organism-centered biology in the early 20th century suffered. Its advocates commonly applied this organizational framework of organisms on highly different units of life, including colonies (Wheeler 1911) and even social states (Hertwig 1922). Especially in holism this problem became most dangerous. For example, holist Adolf Meyer-Abich argued: "From the lion to the termite, every individual organism is always at the same time a member of a supra-individual organism, and the whole difference in this respect between the lion and the termite is only one of the degrees of attachment to the super-organism." (1955, 94; German original). In this sense, both individual organisms and larger groups or colonies share the features of self-organizing and -maintaining wholes. For him, the highest 'organism' is reality itself.

As these cases show, building a framework of the organism solely on this school of thought can blind us from identifying individual organisms at all. One more example will show this: In holobionts (multicellular and multispecies eukaryotes) microbiota are found to be crucial to the organism's development, immune system and metabolic maintenance as a functional physiological unit. The presence of persistent symbionts often plays a role in normal organogenesis and in avoiding harmful autoimmune diseases. Against this background, Scott Gilbert and colleagues (2012) argue, with respect to humans, that 'we have never been individuals.' Instead, we are merely parts in a larger integrated and self-organizing inter-species unit. This shows that you will find individuals (or, depending on your definition, organisms) at whichever level of organization meets the relevant criteria of persistence as functionally integrated and physiological wholes. Every other unit that contributes to this persistence becomes a mere part.[23]

In sum, I am skeptical of the specificity of the persister view. Organisms surely do maintain themselves.[24] But I wonder whether the general properties of self-organization and self-maintenance of organisms are exactly those properties that will allow biologists to single out organisms, rather than any other units,

---

[23] Or one may have to accept the problematic assumption that organisms can be made up of organisms.

[24] Although, in order to understand how organisms (or any living systems) maintain themselves, the concept of maintenance must be broadened again. As Bechtel and Bich (2024) show, it has been narrowed significantly through cybernetics in the 20th century, leading to a view of self-maintenance as negative feedback.

as central explanatory and methodological starting point to study development and evolution. We rather should ask: Are there any relevant features that only organisms have, and other units of life do not? An organism-centered biology should be able to answer this question affirmatively.

This approach has not only the unfortunate consequences that it is endangered of losing grip of the organism and its unique characteristics, but it also cannot clarify why organisms should play a special explanatory role in biology. What is more, it leads to a one-sided understanding of organisms' agency – one that is exclusively shaped by the logic of preservation. It is a logic that is closely linked to Kant's understanding of organismic teleology. Following a critique against Kant already expressed by neo-Kantian Heinrich Rickert, philosopher Georg Toepfer (2024, 222) highlights an important issue: "Following Kant's reasoning, natural teleology is always *preservation teleology*; it is aimed at the conservation of an existing dynamic structure not at its transcending" (emphasis added). In this line of thought, organisms' goals are persisting, sustaining, and maintaining themselves. Organisms are not directly aiming for creative change.

Preservation teleology is common in the above approaches to the organism. In fact, the influential organizational account, which understands itself as being inspired by Kantian ideas, builds its framework of organismal teleology on concepts like 'constraints,' 'closure,' and 'stability.' While this and related accounts, in fact, consider organismal dynamics and variations, like plastic responses to environmental perturbations, these usually only are weighted against the more general goal of preserving the stability of a particular whole. For example, Mossio and colleagues (2016) acknowledge that the organism generates unpredictable variation (functional innovations and organizational variants). But, in the end, the overall system is targeted at preserving useful variations that allows to "realize a new closure through cumulative stability, in which case the functional innovations are integrated into the organization, and preserved" (2016, 33). If organisms, for example, face a "change of constraints, an organized object goes from one closed regime to another, unless the organism does not succeed in establishing a new regime and dies" (Montévil et al. 2016, 47).

In this view, any variation produced by the organism is weighted against (and constrained by) one *larger goal*: to maintain the general metabolic, biochemical, or thermodynamic structure and the global functioning of the system. In teleological terms, organisms only produce variation to find new, innovative ways to maintain themselves. Along similar lines of reasoning, Subrena Smith argues that the "aspect of phenotypic plasticity most pertinent" is "phenotypic accommodation," understood as "the capacity of certain biological systems (those that are organisms) to respond as a whole to environmental contingencies which threaten or promote their persistence" (Smith 2017). In other words, phenotypic plasticity helps to react to environmental challenges to secure the organism's persistence. Thus, there is no room for creative teleological processes directed toward transcending the mere maintenance of biological systems. Organisms' teleological drive, all their agency, activities, and intrinsic purposiveness simply results from obeying their basic physiologically, biochemically, and thermodynamically defined existence.

Organisms may develop various skills for regulating internal processes by anticipating and making-sense of their environment, which allows them to change their organization in different ways and thus to adapt to environmental changes and perturbations, but in all these processes their central goal is to maintain their organization (or organizational closure for that matter) and thus to stay alive:

> [T]he theory of autonomy grounds the purposiveness of adaptive agency, enhanced with sense-making, in terms of the contribution to the intrinsic telos, which is an organized system's own existence. Given that intrinsic purposiveness is *by definition* construed as a circular relation between the existence and the activity of a system, it follows that any function or action performed by an autonomous system is purposive *insofar as* it contributes to determining its conditions of existence. (Virenque and Mossio 2024, 14; emphasis in original)[25]

Several biologists and philosophers within the current debate on an 'Extended Evolutionary Synthesis' have adopted versions of this view of biological agency. For example, Sonia Sultan, Armin Moczek, and Denis Walsh argue:

> Biological agency, in this sense, is the capacity of a system to participate in its own persistence, maintenance, and function by regulating its own structures and activities in response to the conditions it encounters [...]. Agents typically behave in ways that promote the attainment or maintenance of their persistence or viability. (Sultan et al. 2022).

And Kevin Lala and colleagues, referring among others to the work of Erwin Schrödinger, hold:

> Organisms are self-building, self-regulating, highly integrated, functioning, and (crucially) "purposive" wholes, which through wholly natural processes exert a distinctive influence and a degree of control over their own activities, outputs, and local environments. Indeed, organisms *must* have these properties in order to be alive [...]. (Laland et al. 2019, 132; emphasis in original)

I am not saying that this facet of being an agent is not a teleological facet of organisms' existence. In fact, I think it is crucial. But so it is for many

---

[25] See also Nicholson (2018) and Fábregas-Tejeda (2024) who characterized central teleological positions in early 20th century biology in this way.

self-organizing living beings, not only for organisms. In this way, I am questioning whether it can grasp all intrinsic purposiveness that is characteristic of organisms. Are all developmental processes, behaviors, and environmental interactions really directed at this general goal of preservation? Or, at least, what are the unique ways and teleological strategies of organisms that might serve this larger goal of preservation – strategies only they have?

We have seen that there are some shortcomings of past and present theoretical approaches toward the organism and toward highlighting its special role in biology. They concern the way in which the *inward challenge* is addressed. Unfortunately, the historically influential 'persister view' leads to a conceptualization of the organism that loses track of its unique characteristics. It is too general to really grasp the special *organizational dimension* of the organism. This surprisingly leads to an anti-individualistic view of organisms in which they are not highlighted in biology, but become interchangeable units. In addition, this theoretical tradition is threatened to adopt a one-sided view of organisms' teleology and intrinsic purposiveness, in which all goals are identical to those of many (if not all) self-organized living systems. Being guided only by this account might impoverish and bias our understanding and scientific investigation of organismal agency. In other words, while this school of thought commonly aims to highlight the organism in biology, it rather tends to lose it (or to narrow our understanding of it). This tension between defending both individualistic and anti-individualistic perspectives of the organism can also be identified in common solutions to the 'outward challenge.'

Outward Challenge: Reciprocity Ain't Co-constitution

The 'outward challenge' concerns the *relational dimension* of the organism. An organism-centered biology must clarify how we can conceptualize the organism–environment relation in a way that can separate organisms from their environment, even though both are deeply intertwined, and grasp organisms' special purposeful actions in their environments. I will argue that, unfortunately, both early 20th century and current organism-centered biology tend to break down meaningful epistemic boundaries between organisms and environments, and to merge the two units.[26]

To understand this problem, let us recapitulate how these accounts conceptualize the organism–environment relationship. For example, evolutionary biologist Armin Moczek argues:

> We traditionally view the environment as an external agent of selection, one
> that organisms respond to evolutionarily by evolving adaptations, and/or

---

[26] For a more detailed version of this argument, see Baedke et al. (2021).

> developmentally through evolved plastic responses to environmental influ-
> ences [...]. This perspective is challenged by the growing appreciation that
> organisms, rather than adjusting their traits to suit their environment, readily
> alter their environment to suit their traits [...]. (Moczek 2015)

Rather than seeing the environment as an external force imposing unidirectionally selective pressures on passive organisms, several biologists and philosophers of science have recently argued for a shift toward incorporating the idea of 'reciprocal causation' more seriously into biology, especially into evolutionary theory (Mesoudi et al. 2013; Laland et al. 2015; Walsh 2015; for discussion, see Fábregas-Tejeda and Vergara-Silva 2018; Buskell 2019; Baedke et al. 2021; Hazelwood 2023; Baedke and Gilbert 2024). This concept suggests that development and evolution are the result of organism–environment reciprocal interaction.

In recent years, niche construction has become especially important to understand these loops, as it allows organisms to influence the selection pressures acting on them, which allows them to co-shape their evolutionary trajectories. But, as seen above (Section 4.1), this idea has a longer history, being widely defended in early 20th century organism-centered biology, for example, by John Scott Haldane, Jakob von Uexküll, and Conrad Hal Waddington. However, observations of how deeply organisms and environments are interconnected in various contexts has led several of these scholars to argue that it is impossible to separate the two. They contended that the distinction between organism and environment should be abandoned entirely, as it is impossible "to distinguish separately the factors concerned" (Haldane 1935, 12). They thought that life is an 'integrated unity' of organism and environment, which cannot be separated (see Uexküll 1909, 196). In a similar way, Waddington (1957, 189) claimed that "organism and environment are not two separable things." This stance of organism–environment inseparability was built on the idea of ontological co-constitution. Ontological co-constitution holds that organisms and their environments are essentially commingled and form a single interacting system that cannot be meaningfully disentangled (see Haldane 1884, 1935; Levins and Lewontin 1985; Oyama 2000; Griffiths and Gray 2001; Walsh 2015, 2022; for discussion, see Baedke 2019a; Pearce 2020). In contrast, reciprocal causation is usually defined as a feedback loop between two interacting, yet separate entities or processes.

The same tendency to reinterpret reciprocal causation as co-constitution can be found in the current 'return of the organism' in which biologists and philosophers increasingly reject the idea of a boundary between organism and environment.[27] In this movement, reciprocity has emerged as a key theoretical

---

[27] For an in-depth discussion of the relations and boundaries between organism and environment, see Fábregas-Tejeda (forthcoming).

and modeling principle, supported by its apparent empirical relevance, with the assertion that reciprocal interactions are widespread in evolutionary processes. In this account, several authors have argued that one cannot identify unambiguous and consistent boundaries between organisms and environments. Especially in the field of niche construction theory, views of co-constitution are often built on developmental systems theory and its assumption that "[t]here is no distinction between organism and environment" (Griffiths and Gray 2001, 207). Like earlier ideas by Haldane and his contemporaries, some accounts of niche construction highlight the importance of the organism in evolution, but, at the same time, merge organisms with environments.

For example, Sonia Sultan (2015) argues that it is challenging to define a clear boundary between organism and environment, as "individual phenotypes inevitably affect both the external environment and the organism's experience of that environment" (44–45).[28] She draws on the case of pregnant meadow voles (*Microtus pennsylvanicus*) that alter hormonal signals in their offspring in response to changing day length. Then, autumn-born pups develop thicker coats than summer-born ones, which in turn affects how they experience and interact with their environment. Sultan argues that in such cases of reciprocal influence the organism–environment distinction becomes questionable. This critique echoes Uexküll's (1909, 196) earlier view that organisms and environments form an 'inextricable whole', since organisms' 'perception world' and 'effect world' are deeply interconnected. In a similar way, Walsh (2022) claims that when an organism and environment mutually influence each other, the system cannot be explained by separating the effects of each, resulting in an inseparable dynamic. Yet others have argued recently, in a similar way, that "it is not possible to distinguish what is 'biological' from what is environmental/cultural" (Laland and Brown 2018, 127).

Unfortunately, these arguments for organism–environment co-constitution create a conceptual rift within approaches toward an organism-centered biology. On the one hand, they aim to highlight the organism as crucial autonomous and active unit that causes developmental and evolutionary change by co-constructing its environment. On the other hand, they often conceptualize the organism as inextricably interwoven and indistinguishable from its environment. The latter tendency opens the door for unwanted anti-individualistic views of the organism that threaten attempts to consolidate the position of the organism in biology.[29]

---

[28] This Element most widely excludes the complex issue of organismal experience. For recent accounts that argue for the necessity to include an experiential side to niche construction to understand purposive behavior of organisms in evolution, see Sultan (2015), Chiu (2019), and Baedke et al. (2021).

[29] For a detailed discussion of the problems going along with the views of organism–environment co-constitution or inseparability and the tendency of merging the two components, see Baedke (2019a), Baedke et al. (2021).

In addition, one may wonder if this view of inseparability actually solves the central problem of individuation of biological units. As already Joseph Needham (1936, 10–11) highlighted against such views in the early 20th century, claiming that the organism and environment form an inseparable unit still carries the burden of demonstrating how to individuate such a larger system. How do we differentiate the organism–environment system from other systems? Individuation is still essential for distinguishing between the proximal and distal environments of a given system (i.e., which elements of the physical world are part of that system and which not). According to Needham, biologists need clear individuation criteria to carry on their research, otherwise they are unable to tell apart environmental features relevant to the organism from those irrelevant to it.

In sum, we see that also in past and present attempts to address the *outward challenge* something is wanting. Too often attempts to highlight the organism and its creative actions and relations to its environment end up dissolving the organism in its surrounding. In contrast, an organism-centered biology should be able to avoid such a position.

Consequences

The ability to identify and conceptually grasp relevant units in nature has wide-ranging consequences for biological research. This includes issues like which questions scientists ask (or not ask), what theories they develop, how they model phenomena, which variables they choose, what model organism they select, and so forth. These practical consequences become most apparent when individuating organisms. We need a clear understanding of what organisms are, how they are organized and how they interact with an environment different from them in order to characterize relevant units of physiological change and ecological interaction, to recognize which biological systems can legitimately be considered 'causal agents,' to distinguish between one or more conspecifics in a community or population, and for individuating the organismal partners in multispecies collectives such as holobionts.

Unfortunately, both solutions to the inside and outside challenge discussed do not successfully address the problem of individuating organisms, but rather push it aside: One by treating organisms as too similar to other living systems, the other by merging it with its environment. Both positions can easily lead to methodological problems as the organism becomes intractable or harder to assay in empirical studies. In addition, blurring the boundaries of the organism may lead to the problem that results become harder to translate into experimental interventions. For example, merging the physiological units of mother, microbes and fetus in one inextricable unit (Gilbert 2014), may pose problems of how to target each of these interacting partners individually in the case of heath interventions.

In evolutionary research, modeling practices are complicated by conceptual ambiguities about the unit of the individual organism. For example, not being able to identify individual organisms in evolutionary biology makes it difficult to count individuals in populations (Okasha forthcoming), to identify parent-offspring relations, and to ultimately measure reproduction rates and population dynamics. For example, the boundaries we draw to identify organisms in cases such as epigenetic inheritance and niche construction directly influence how we model and measure these units' ecological and evolutionary influences. This means that taking divergent individualistic or anti-individualistic perspectives on the organism affects what is considered relevant and irrelevant (background) variables in models, and, finally, what is considered as a (possibly) cause or an effect. As another example, Evo-Devo needs to be able to clearly show how organisms modulate, bias, and possibly guide the production of variation, from developmental constraints to plasticity, in ways that are unique to these units and different from, say, how cells affect the production of variation in multicellular species. In addition, niche construction theory should be able to clearly individuate the organism and its causal roles if it wants to study this unit as an autonomous causal agent, different from its environment, which actively molds its own niche, and thus leads to evolutionary consequences and environments that differ from those in which organismal agents are not involved.

In more general words, an organism-centered biology needs to be able to empirically and methodologically secure the special role of the organism. This includes its unique causal status as a goal-directed and active agential 'nexus' that exerts control over itself and its environment, and its unique epistemic status of allowing scientists to explain and understand crucial developmental, physiological, ecological, and evolutionary processes. Empirical and philosophical work needs to show that the ideas of organismal organization and organism–environment reciprocity are in fact able to highlight the organism as identifiable driver of development and evolution, without losing it as a causally efficacious and autonomous unit. I now develop the first draft of a conceptual framework that leads into this direction.

4.3 New Solutions: Organisms as Overcomers and Agents in the Environment

Let us take the above two shortcomings of prevailing accounts as a starting point to develop a new understanding of the organism. A theoretical framework that does not fall prey to anti-individualistic perspectives and is precise enough to act as a conceptual foundation for an organism-centered biology of the 21st century. This is a major endeavor, one that can hardly be developed in this Element alone. But let me at least outline the basic features of this framework, its premises, and consequences. It has two components: one concerns the organizational dimension of the organism, the other its relational one.

The Organizational Dimension of the Organism

Let us first deal with the organizational dimension: The account that I will defend understands organisms not *only* as 'persisters' that maintain themselves. Organisms are also 'overcomers.' What characterizes an organism as an overcomer? I will first develop central theoretical components of this view and then exemplify them by drawing on three empirical cases.

The organizational account presupposes that when variation is introduced in organisms this transition leads from one organized state (a closed regime) to another. In this transition, the organism might succeed in reaching the other state of closure or fail to reach it. In the latter case, the organism dies. During a successful transition, the organism's "closure is always met, even though the constraints relevant to closure may and do change" (Montévil et al. 2016, 47). In some cases, new variations may be rejected by the existing organizational regime in order to avoid destabilization and death. Other variations are maintained and integrated into the organization, then gain a function in a new regime (e.g., in the mammalian life cycle, lungs are first developed and maintained, then acquire a function after birth in a new organizational setting). Yet other variations destabilize the whole organization in such a way that the organism dies. As an example of the latter scenario, Montévil and colleagues (2016) discuss carcinomas, which lead to a progressive disorganization of the tissue and, sometimes, to a disruption of the organisms' whole organization and its death.

The overcomer view understands the introduction of new variation and the process of organizational transitions differently. It suggests, first, that in organisms destabilization does not necessarily lead to a trajectory toward death. Instead, organisms show a characteristic set of dynamics – deorganization and reorganization – that is a non-pathological component of their development and life cycles. This includes, second, that organisms can actively and creatively tinker with their own organization by destabilizing it. As we will see, organisms often actively give up their organization during developmental or evolutionary phases to become qualitatively different functional wholes. Third, this view does not presuppose that "organisms change while staying organized" (Montévil et al. 2016, 49), that is, as a continuous series of states of closure.

In fact, they sometimes change by actively destabilizing themselves and their closure. This may be a risky move, but one that can be highly rewarding.

This means that organisms do not always stick to the same rules under which a given functional wholeness is maintained. They can change these rules, deconstruct their wholeness, reject closure, and reorganize themselves during development. I suggest that not all living systems – all persisters – are able to actively tinker in this way with themselves and with their own organization, respectively. Only organisms can. They have developed special agential strategies to induce, modulate, and control phases of destabilized organization. These agential abilities can especially be observed in situations where the organism faces environmental challenges. Let us have a look at three cases that exemplify these characteristics of organisms as overcomers.

1) *Immunity in deep-sea anglerfish*: Vertebrates, including humans, have two types of immune systems. The first, the innate system, reacts quickly to microscopic invaders using barriers like skin and cells (macrophages). The second is the adaptive system, which uses "killer" T cells and antibodies to destroy pathogens and to target-specific bacteria or viruses. Both systems work together to protect against infections and disease. In some species of deep-sea anglerfish, when two organisms mate, they completely delete their organization as an immunological self and fuse together as one unit in which males are permanently attached to host females (Swann et al. 2020; see Figure 6A).

   While all vertebrates have two immune systems, several taxa of anglerfish are able to completely deorganize and delete one of them, namely their adaptive immune system. This allows the temporary or permanent fusion of tissues of two individuals without triggering an immune response. They then form a new metabolic and morphological whole with one respiratory and digestive system. These fish have traded their immune protection – losing genes that control their adaptive immune system, including production of antibodies and T cell compartment – to reach a completely new metabolic and morphological organization with reproductive advantages. The male clamps his teeth onto a part of the female and stays put, and eventually the skins of male and female grow together, and blood vessels do too. This fusion is a reaction to the challenges posed when finding a mate in a vast and mostly empty environment. In fact, ca. 30 percent of all females never encounter a mate and remain solitary without reproduction throughout their life (Pietsch 2009) – with a highly deconstructed immune system.

   Importantly, current studies also suggest that the evolution from temporary to permanent attachment of the male included already in temporary forms the loss of genes that play crucial roles in the vertebrate immune

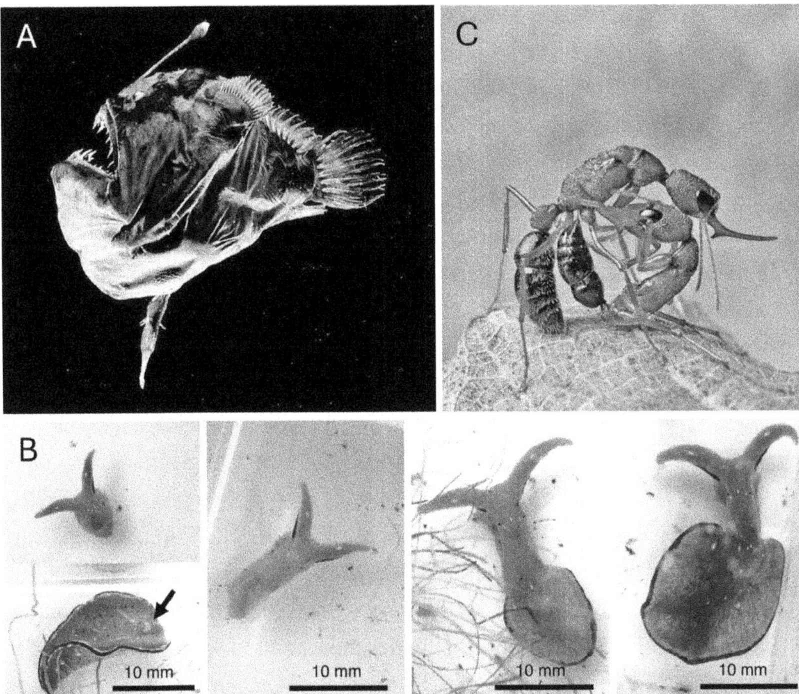

Figure 6 Three examples of organisms as overcomers. (A) Female deep-sea anglerfish (*Melanocetus johnsonii*) with an attached male. (B) Autotomy and regeneration in sea slugs (*Elysia marginata*): head and body just after autotomy (left pictures; arrow highlights heart) and regeneration on day 7, day 14, and full regeneration at day 22 (next three pictures from left). (C) Workers of Indian jumping ants (*Harpegnathos saltator*) fighting in dominance tournament that induces gamergates. For description, see text. (A: Photograph reproduced with permission of Edith A. Widder. B: Mitoh and Yusa 2021, reproduced with permission of Elsevier; C: Photograph by Kalyan Varma, reproduced with permission of Wikipedia).

system (Swann et al. 2020). It is a highly risky move to tinker with the immune system in such ways, to deorganize it without clearly foreseeable functionality and to curtail allogeneic reactions. But this temporary distortion of organization, in this case, opened up new forms of life cycles with permanent pairing and completely new reproductive strategies. It also shows that, in contrast to the commonly assumed stability and fixity of the coevolved connection between innate and adaptive immune systems in vertebrates, there is a surprising degree of evolvability in these systems, a 'risky' space of phenotypic possibilities organisms actively explore.

2) *Autotomy in sea slugs*: Some sea slug species (e.g., *Elysia marginata*) can 'decapitate' themselves within the course of several hours, separating their head from the rest of the body. This behavior is known as autotomy. Surprisingly, the single heads do not die. Instead, within twenty days, they regenerate an entirely new body, while the former body dies (Mitoh and Yusa 2021; see Figure 6B). During this time, the sea slug head neither has a heart, a digestive tract, nor other vital organs. However, the head is able to move autonomously and, in young individuals, starts to feed on algae within a few hours. Heads of older sea slugs seemingly do not feed and die within ten days after separating from their body.

It is suggested that these sacoglossans obtain energy for survival and regeneration from photosynthesis by integrating the chloroplasts of algae into their tissue (a phenomenon known as 'kleptoplasty'), even though they cannot digest this food. Autotomy in these sea slug species is possibly a process to eliminate parasites on the body. Together with the observation that chloroplast concentration can change during the lifetime of sea slugs with kleptoplasty (e.g., sea slugs lose chloroplasts when starved; Shiroyama et al. 2020), this suggests that there might exist specific environmentally dependent and life-phase sensitive tactics controlling the onset of kleptoplasty and autotomy. In sum, while the underlying mechanisms of autotomy in this species needs to be studied in detail, this case shows that organisms even can completely deconstruct their metabolic organization (losing the main body including heart) and survive this procedure.

3) *Pseudo-queens in Indian jumping ants*: In many insect societies, the death of a queen leads to the collapse of the colony. However, the colonies of Indian jumping ants (*Harpegnathos saltator*) follow a different path. When their queen dies, certain worker ants engage in ritualized battles to determine who will take over as a 'pseudo-queen,' or so-called 'gamergate' (Penick et al. 2021; see Figure 6C). When the queen is alive, her pheromones suppress egg-laying in workers, but her absence triggers a dominance tournament among the workers, which can go on for up to a month. This combat, which includes antennal dueling and biting, produces gamergates, with significantly changed organization. They reduce their brain volume by 20 percent, significantly change their behavior (from aggressive hunters that leave the nest to egg-layers that no longer leave the nest and hide from intruders), their venom glands recede, they expand their ovaries to five times their original size, and exhibit different gene expression profiles. Their lifespan also increases from about six months to three years or more.

These workers completely reorganize their metabolic system (e.g., energy originally used for large brains is saved) to develop an entirely new ability: reproduction. Interestingly, this plastic ability is reversible. Gamergates may lose their status, for example, when isolated from the colony. In this case, their bodies quickly revert to their previous state as workers. They even regrow their brains, against the typical wisdom that brain cells once lost do not come back.

What do these cases tell us about organisms' status as overcomers?

➤ First, in addition to maintaining their organizational closure, organisms are open and ready for substantial distortion of their organization. Their immunological, metabolic, and reproductive systems are likely more flexible than previously assumed. Besides normal variation introduced, organisms may allow for variation that is risky, which means that it might distort the whole organization of organisms and (over a certain developmental or evolutionary time) decrease organism–environment matching (e.g., anglerfish are less protected from infections, sea slugs can no longer digest algae). Some of this variation might bring organisms closer to thermodynamic equilibrium and death, respectively. From this perspective, the first two of the three cases could be considered more risky forms of destabilized organization than the last one.

➤ Second, the initiated phase of instability opens up a new space of phenotypic variation and unexplored life cycles characteristics that organisms can explore (new reproductive strategies in anglerfish and ants and new endosymbiotic forms of energy production in sea slugs). Organisms have abilities to endure, at least for some time, in such phases of instability and find solutions in creative ways to acquire new developmentally and evolutionary stable forms of organization, and thus to be able to leave these phases again.

➤ Third, overcoming is not the same as persisting and organisms differ from merely self-maintaining systems. For instance, the colony of Indian jumping ants is a functionally immortal persister. It changes its organization of parts and constraints (workers take over roles of the dead queen), but always persists as a whole (reproductive) unit. Instead, the individual ants substantially change their whole organization and actively explore a whole new life cycle (they reproduce) with a radically different transgenerational impact. This fundamental organizational shift in the organism is, in fact, not directed towards the 'larger' goal of maintaining the individual ant or at its ongoing existence, but towards the persistence of the whole colony, which however is not an organism. Thus, we should keep the two modes of persisting and overcoming apart if we want to grasp these fine distinctions and to differentiate these two kinds of systems.

In sum, we come to see that organisms do profoundly more than simply maintaining their organizational closure far from thermodynamic equilibrium. They also sometimes actively change by destabilizing themselves and rejecting their particular forms of closure. They are creative agents that possess genetic, developmental and behavioral repertoires and strategies to modulate and tinker with this organization, push it toward instability, control and maintain these instable periods, and then stir instability toward the production of stabilizing and possibly adaptive variation. They may fail in this process or may succeed. If they succeed, this may open up new trajectories that are especially relevant for studies in developmental evolution, like plasticity-led evolution.

While self-organized persistence surely can generate evolutionary relevant and adaptive variation itself, I suggest that substantial change in life cycles and evolutionary novelties might often be introduced by overcomers and their more comprehensive organizational transitions. For example, the above few cases alone show how overcomers are involved in the evolution of novelties in the immune system in vertebrates, in the evolution of endosymbiosis, the evolution of reproductive strategies in colonies, and the evolution of reversible phenotypic plasticity.[30] What is more, the conceptual framework of the overcomer could point us toward medically relevant properties of organisms' organization. The mentioned three cases alone might open up new avenues to treat histoincompatibility of tissues, to develop transplantation techniques and approaches in regenerative medicine, and to explore new ways to enhance brain plasticity in humans.

I suggest that organisms' abilities as overcomers are far more common across the tree of life than one might assume. In fact, there are several similar phenomena: injured comb jellies (ctenophores) can merge to form one individual with one integrated digestive tract and nervous system, which shows that these last common ancestors of animals are way more plastic than previously assumed (Jokura et al. 2024). In addition, comprehensive forms of regenerative deorganizations can not only be found in animals but plants, too, like autotomy in the South African plant *Oxalis pes-caprae*, which involves the herbivory-induced sacrifice of vital organs in order to prevent the uprooting of the whole plant (Shtein et al. 2019). The abilities of overcomers might actually be widespread in plants due to their modular construction. For example, developmental instability has long been studied in plants (Polak 2003; Forde 2009; Nuche et al. 2014). The ways this

---

[30] One may also suggest that the overcomer view points toward developmental and evolutionary shifts in the individuality of organisms (see also Kingma 2020). Overcomers often change their organization in ways that allow them to switch from being, for example, a metabolically integrated individual to an ecologically integrated one (sea slug with symbionts), or from a physiological to a reproductive individual (ants). In this way, organisms seem to explore different facets of their organizational and relational dimension in phases of instability.

instability is produced and controlled, how it leads to substantial changes in plants' 'body plans' and structural patterns, and how it affects plant performance and fitness could be another good starting point to explore organisms' characteristics as overcomers. More generally, still today, many forms of plasticity, intraindividual variation and microheterogeneity in organisms cannot be observed in the lab due to various constraining, standardizing, and stabilizing procedures. Thus, suitable methodologies need to be developed that allow organisms to display the potential range of variation they can produce and instability they can overcome.

The three case studies discussed above all include quite substantial environmental challenges. However, while such special contexts allow triggering organisms' abilities as overcomers in easier ways, I suggest that organisms explore the limits of their own organization also in less radical environmental settings. In any case, the framework of the overcomer introduces different understandings not only of the organizational dimension of the organism but also of the environment. Here environments are not limited to mere background conditions that provide a repertoire of energetic resources or challenges for the organism to meet the central goal of maintaining its internal closure and far-from-equilibrium thermodynamic state, as usually assumed in organizational approaches (e.g., Moreno and Mossio 2015: Ch. 4).[31]

Instead, in the present account the organism–environment relation has a more active and broader character (including not only the parts of the environment that are relevant for organisms' self-maintenance). While organisms as overcomers react to environments and are sensitive to changes in their surroundings, they also *inter*act with it, construct and harness it, and even integrate it when tinkering with their own internal organization, in ways not always linked to their persistence. For example, in the three cases discussed, developmental, physiological and evolutionary change was linked to a complex web of active interactions between organisms as reproductive partners, symbiotic partners, and ecological partners of a larger collective, and their associated abiotic factors. This means that, by tinkering with *external* relations, organisms change *internal* organizations, and *vice versa*. In this sense, the overcomer view is not blind to the relational dimension of the nexus concept of the organism. Instead: Changes in relations and organizations go hand in hand.

---

[31] In addition, for example, Mossio and Bich (2017, 1098) express this view: "Unlike the evolutionary approach, the organisational one puts more emphasis on the internal dimension of living systems rather than on external influences, by focusing mainly on physiology. In this way, the organisational approach takes into consideration the relation between organism and environment as it unfolds in the present, in terms of internal compensations for environmental perturbations."

The Relational Dimension of the Organisms

Let us now focus on said relational dimension of the organism in detail. The account developed here presupposes that despite complex reciprocal relations between organisms and environments in developmental, ecological, and evolutionary settings, organisms and their causal roles can be unambiguously identified and distinguished from the environment. In other words, we can secure the idea, central for an organism-centered biology, that organisms are not only products but also causes of evolution as well as distinct creative agents that drive evolutionary trajectories. This view implies that we do not have to seek shelter from complex feedback loops by drawing on the idea of organism–environment co-constitution or by merging the two units. Instead, we can maintain meaningful epistemic boundaries between organisms and environments.

To develop this position, let me draw on a conceptual and visual model of reciprocal causation model developed with Alejandro Fábregas-Tejeda and Guido Prieto (Baedke et al. 2021). It should be applicable to a diversity of different forms of niche construction (see Aaby and Ramsey 2022; Chiu 2019). This includes, for example, cases of external or physical niche construction (organisms modify factors in their external environments; e.g., soil-processing earthworms) or relational niche construction (a change in the relations between organisms and environments without transforming organisms' constitution nor the physical conditions of their environment; e.g., mice that pile up to keep warm by affecting the rates of heat loss due to physical proximity, but without changing the actual physical temperature of the nest). The aim of this model is to disentangle seemingly inextricable reciprocal relations by identifying characteristic causal patterns of different evolutionary relevant organism–environment interactions.

A basic assumption of this framework is that we do not have to represent organism and environment as partaking in a seemingly inextricable reciprocal loop (see Figure 7A; see also Di Paolo 2020), which, as we have seen, has led to various claims of organism–environment inseparability from the early 20th century until today. To begin unknotting the reciprocal interactions between organism and environment, we must first distinguish the two components. This means recognizing that some causal processes in the organism are relatively independent of the environment, and vice versa. Beyond causal links between organism and environment, we must also account for internal processes that occur solely within each unit (Figure 7B). With respect to organisms, this may include processes in which organisms maintain their internal organization (as persisters) or destabilize their internal organization (as overcomers) given particular environmental influences. However, at this stage we still face a conceptual challenge,

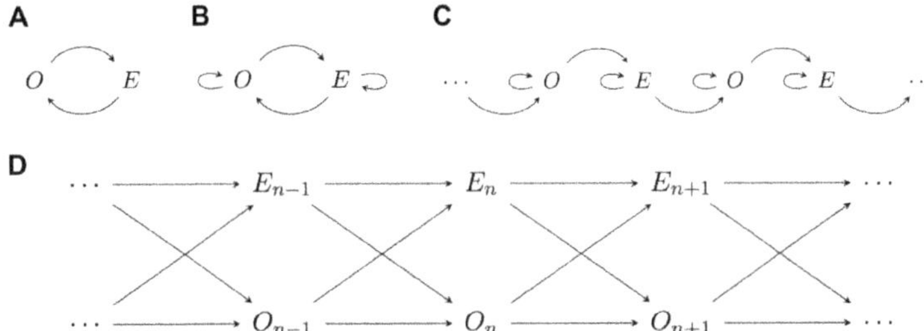

Figure 7 Unknotting organism–environment reciprocal causation. (A) Organism (O) and environment (E) engage in a reciprocal interaction loop. (B) Additional loops represent internal causal processes within organism and environment; for the organism, this concerns processes of persisting and overcoming. (C) Sequential depiction of the organism–environment interactions from (B). (D) Model of reciprocal causation showing a progression of states, with subscripts indicating organism and environment states, and arrows representing causal influences (see Baedke et al. 2021).

as simple loop representations do not capture how these causal interactions unfold over time. The next step is to unroll the organism–environment cycle to show the sequential nature of their reciprocal causation (see Figure 7C). By considering organism and environment as distinct entities, we can better articulate how their complex causal relations unfold over organisms' life histories.

To really grasp the reciprocal interaction of organism and environment, our model suggest adopting a slightly refined version of this 'open-loop' version (see Figure 7D) that includes two ordered series of organism and environment states (O and E) and arrows representing causal processes within and between them. For example, the interaction between organism and environment at state n (symbolized as O_n and E_n) causally influences the next state of organism, the environment, or both (O_{n+1} and E_{n+1}). The model represents these causal links, and when fully mapped, the unknotted network of organism–environment reciprocity (see Figure 7D).[32] However, the model only becomes insightful when we emphasize the most relevant causal arrows for a given explanation. This highlights the key causal pathways, that is, invariant paths, between changes in organism and environment states, while allowing us to abstract away from less relevant interactions. It is important to remember that even when certain pathways are not emphasized (e.g., they are not included in an explanation of a phenomenon), all causal relations are always in effect.

---

[32] In this model, the causal relations between, for example, an organism state and a later environment state can be understood as being invariant under a range of counterfactual interventions on the organism state (see Woodward 2003).

Let me briefly exemplify how this model helps us identifying and disentangling the causal influences of interacting partners in a reciprocal loop of niche construction. For instance, reef-building corals significantly change their environments by secreting calcium carbonate skeletons, which accumulate to form complex habitats for numerous species (Jones et al. 1994). These environmental changes reciprocally affect the corals. For example, macroalgae and sponges that settle on reefs compete with corals for space, light, or food (see Sultan 2015). This case of niche construction is illustrated in Figure 8A (sequence 1–3). Corals (O_{n-1}) in an aquatic environment (E_{n-1}) secrete calcium carbonate, which (1) changes the species composition of the environment in state (E_n), that now includes new competitors for the corals (O_n). These competitors (2) impact coral survival, development, or reproduction at the next coral state (O_{n+1}). Corals may then (3) respond by modifying the environment in another niche construction cycle.

This simple model can be applied to more complex cases where the individual contributors are seemingly harder to disentangle. An interesting case is the transition to herbivory in ruminants and the role of symbiotic microbes in it (Chiu and Gilbert 2020; Gilbert 2020). This involves two processes. First, microbes colonize the animal's digestive system and help develop the rumen, their habitat. Second, this development shifts the animal's diet to herbivory,

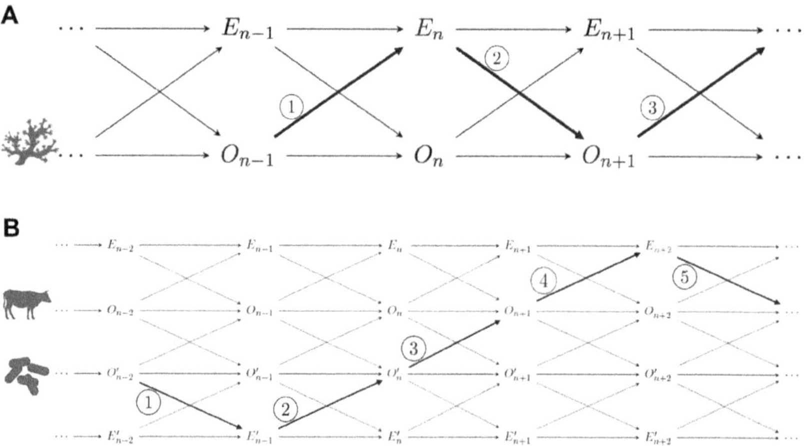

Figure 8 Application of the model on two examples of reciprocal niche construction. (A) Causal diagram for niche construction in reef-building corals; highlighted arrows trace a causal path aligned with steps (1–3). (B) Causal diagram of the transition to herbivory in ruminants (O) in a given environment (E). This transition is in part explained by changes in the rumen (E') caused by microbes (O'), which allow animal experience to feed on plants (E). For details, see text. (Figure modified after Baedke et al. 2021).

enabling it to perceive and treat plants as food.[33] Chiu and Gilbert argue that ruminants also engage in niche construction by co-shaping their microbiota's niche and that (b) the holobiont (ruminant host and microbes) acts as a single unit experiencing and acting on the environment. However, these two claims taken together are problematic because (a) treats microbes and host as separate units, while (b) assumes they function as one unified system.

Our model can bring some clarify to this case (see Figure 8B, sequence 1–5). It treats rumen microbes (O') and the animal host (O) as distinct organisms. The microbiome's environment is the rumen (E'), while the host's environment is its external environment (E). After colonizing the rumen at birth, microbes (O'_{n-2}) proliferate and release compounds that trigger rumen growth and differentiation (1). The modified rumen (E'_{n-1}) then promotes further microbial proliferation and diversity (2). This evolving microbiome affects the animal's constitution (3), leading the host to perceive plants as digestible and start feeding on them. This herbivory can have downstream effects on ecosystems (4). This dietary change and new form of interaction with the environment alters the animal's development (5), which, in turn, impacts the rumen microbiome's diversity and composition (not depicted). Further reciprocal processes include microbes that continue to mold the rumen which, for example, leads to the animal's ability to neutralizing toxic plant defenses.

Applying our model to this case shows that understanding niche construction requires treating microbes as organisms distinct from their host and studying their reciprocal interactions with their environments separately. Viewing the holobiont as a single unit – merging different organisms, ruminant, and microbes – would obscure the microbes' niche construction activities. We would not be able to identify their constructive organismal activities, simply because we would only be left with the environment of the holobiont (not of microbes). Thus, the 'holobiont-as-individual' approach would collapse the microbial role to microbes' effects on this external environment, impoverishing the analysis to only part of the process (i.e., steps 3–5).

In sum, this framework allows drawing epistemically meaningful boundaries between organism and environment, instead of blurring their relations which would lead to each component's intractability for empirical studies. It effectively captures and distinguishes different causal pathways of reciprocal interacting units, reveals their unique patterns and incorporates them into complex evolutionary scenarios that were previously difficult to grasp. These scenarios often involve multispecies interactions with different forms of niche construction. However,

---

[33] In the following, for the sake of simplicity, I abstract from the experiential component of this case. For a detailed discussion, see Baedke et al. (2021).

even in these complex cases we do not need to assume organism–environment inseparability or co-constitution. Instead, by clarifying these dynamics, we can conceptualize the organism and the environment as distinct contributors to shared pathways. What is more, the internal logic of the model also paves the way for formalizing reciprocal organism–environment interactions, as it can easily be translated into, for example, causal graph theory (Otsuka 2015).

I would like to highlight that this model does not imply that the relationship between organisms and environments are perfectly symmetrical. Rather, while they are reciprocal, they usually are asymmetrical. The causal profile of the modifications that organisms exert on their environments differs from how environmental causes affect organisms (see Fábregas-Tejeda forthcoming). Usually, organisms affect their environments as clearly bounded loci of causation, as agents that set specific goals, like maintaining or overcoming their organization, reproduction, and so forth. They exert a specific kind of control over the realization of these goals through targeted developmental and behavioral repertoires. In contrast, as Alejandro Fábregas-Tejeda argues, environments are rather causally dispersed and fragmented units, as they constitute a highly heterogeneous set of various biotic and abiotic factors that affect only certain developmental or physiological processes of the organism during particular life phases. In short, the organismal environment should not be understood as a bounded causal unit targeted at one shared goal. Therefore, in reciprocal processes of niche construction, we usually find a particular kind of *asymmetrical* relationship. In this asymmetrical connection organisms as agents are crucial driving forces, that, through their intrinsic purposiveness and repertoires to exert control over themselves and their surroundings, bias or direct the future dynamics and trajectories of the organism–environment link.

We now have identified the necessary ingredients for our conceptual framework to suitably grasp the organism (see Box 3).

Box 3 Toward a new framework of the organism.

➤ Organisms exhibit an organizational and a relational dimension. The first concerns organisms' internal structure and the second their relations to the environment. Both dimensions are distinct, but strongly affect one another.

➤ The *organizational dimension* of the organism includes two components: organisms are (i) 'persisters': they maintain themselves as organized wholes. Organisms share this characteristic with many other living beings. They are also (ii) 'overcomers': they have special

---

Box 3 (cont.)

strategies to induce, modulate, and exert control over phases of destabilized organization. Especially this second characteristic allows them to introduce and maintain qualitatively novel variation during life cycles and in evolution. The agential abilities of overcomers can especially be observed in situations where the organism faces environmental challenges and shifts.

➤ Organisms' control over their internal organization depends on their active interaction with their environment. Thus, environments are not merely background conditions.

➤ The *relational dimension* of the organism includes different ecological and evolutionary forms of organism–environment interaction. Often, this interaction is reciprocal. Organisms are affected by their biotic and abiotic environment, but they also co-construct this environment.

➤ We can identify organisms in complex webs of reciprocal organism–environment relations by tracing (causal patterns of) their diachronic influences during these interactions. In addition, by identifying them as bounded loci of causation, as agents, we can recognize that they impose an asymmetrical causal structure on organism–environment relations.

➤ In sum, organisms are a special kind of living beings that are able to actively and creatively tinker with themselves and with their environment in ways that allow them to maintain themselves and to explore new developmental and evolutionary pathways and forms of existence.

In this Element, the central ideas of this conceptual framework can only be drawn with rough brushstrokes. The same hold for its consequences: This view of the organism helps overcoming past anti-individualistic tendencies of other theories of the organism, especially those central for organism-centered biology in the early 20th century and for the current 'return of the organism.' While other views paradoxically tend to lose the unit of the organism, the present approach highlights it. It also avoids a common theoretical bias to focus on only one of the two dimensions of the organism: organizational *or* relational. Instead, this account suggests that to grasp the complex characteristics of organisms an integrated view bridging both dimensions is strongly needed. In addition, it acknowledges the special agential roles organisms play in development and evolution. Organisms actively bias and shape their developmental pathways, physiological structures, metabolic and immunological states, environmental niches, ecological interactions, and the strength and direction of selection pressures that can affect population dynamics.

François Jacob (1977) famously said that evolution 'tinkers' with existing building blocks of living systems to create adaptations. Instead, the present framework suggests that actually organisms are the tinkerers. They tinker with their own organismal constitution and environmental settings. By doing so, they significantly contribute to the production, maintenance and selection of variation in evolution. In contrast to natural selection, that, understood as a tinkerer, has no specific end in mind, the organism tinkers by having several goals 'in mind' – some are more clearly set (survival, reproducing), while others make necessary more creative and explorative modes of tinkering (producing novel variation given environmental challenges), and yet others need to be coordinated with other organisms (reproductive and ecological partners) and their goals.

This framework, I conclude, restores organisms as (possibly) the most central unit in biology – as an epistemic focal point any organism-centered biology can be built upon. In addition, it stirs biology to a set of highly relevant, but still little understood phenomena where organisms are causal centers and active 'tinkerers' at the interface of development and evolution, like developmental constraints, plasticity-led evolution, and niche construction. Besides this centrality of the organism in biology, this concept also plays crucial roles in society. Let us have a closer look at these roles now.

5 The Organism and Human Life

The developmental and theoretical biologist Paul A. Weiss once said:

> Biology has made spectacular advances by adopting the disciplined methods of the inorganic sciences and mathematics, but it has not widened its conceptual framework in equal measure. [. . .] [B]iology must retain the courage of its own insights into living nature; for after all, organisms are not just heaps of molecules. At least, I cannot bring myself to feel like one. Can you? (Weiss 1969, 42)

Weiss points toward an important issue – the fact that the units of biological investigation, and especially the organism, are always linked to anthropological and social perspectives. They deeply shape the way we understand ourselves as humans and our relationship to others. When it comes to the organism concept, this is possible due to its characteristics as (i) a highly flexible nexus concept whose organizational and relational dimensions can be used in various ways to stimulate anthropological and sociopolitical debates (e.g., using the organisms as an analogy to understand the structure of a state) and as (ii) a biological counterpart to concepts with societal relevance, like person, individual, and body. Therefore, let us have a brief look at how the concept of the organism shapes our life. While there are more issues one could discuss here, let us focus on two crucial ones: freedom or self-determination, on the one hand, and race and racism on the other.

In the 20th century the two central units of biological investigations – the gene and populations – were at the center of larger public debates about humans' biological constitution and relations. In its most radical form, genes have been used to defend a position of genetic determinism, most prominently in the field of sociobiology. Gene determinism suggests that peoples' personality or behavior is primarily determined by their genetic makeup, rather than by social or cultural influences. This position was sometimes linked with the view that basically 'you are your genes.' Throughout the century, gene determinism was used to legitimize cruelties like involuntary sterilizations and genocides.

However, in the past twenty years, this view of people as fixed 'vehicles' for genetic programs has come under attack with the rise of postgenomics (Stotz 2008; Richardson and Stevens 2015). Postgenomics reconceptualizes development and inheritance as multifactorial relationships between environmental factors, developmental mechanisms, and the genome. Thus, how and when genetic information is relevant, is no longer determined intrinsically but rather by the genes' organismal and extraorganismal environment. Fields like epigenetics, microbiome science, metabolomics, nutrigenomics, and the developmental origins of health and disease framework (DOHaD) now highlight individuals' material and social environments (e.g., life styles, stress, nutritional habits, and income) as central causes for humans' ontogenetic and even transgenerational destinies. They conceptualize diseases like type-2 diabetes, metabolic syndrome, cancer, and autism, as instances of social and environmental 'programming.' This new view has a focus on the flexibility of the organism–environment relation and on developmental plasticity. It holds potential for disrupting previous genetic determinist thinking, especially in debates about the nature of the human body. For example, Jörg Niewöhner (2011) suggests that based on organismal perspectives in postgenomics the concept of the 'embedded body' is emerging in the life sciences. According to this concept, bodies are not machine-like, genetically programmed entities, but open, dynamic systems, deeply interconnected with their material and social surroundings (see Baedke 2017). In this account, the individual is often depicted as freed from the 'chains of its genes' (see Pickersgill et al. 2013) and liberated to live a life that guarantees humans 'plastic' destiny, autonomy, and self-determination.

At the same time, however, these new developments toward the organism have introduced deterministic or reductionist narratives of their own (Richardson et al. 2014; Waggoner and Uller 2015; Baedke et al. 2023–2025). New forms of 'postgenomic determinism' and environmental determinism emerged, for example, in the field of epigenetics, where parents' decision-making and their socio-economic 'niche' is considered to irreversibly damage the development of their children (and further generations). This motive is expressed, for example, in newspaper headlines such as "Babies born into poverty are damaged forever before birth" (McLaughlin 2012). This development also includes an overemphasis on the causal role of mothers as the most central public health care agents who are increasingly considered accountable and guilty for the health or diseases of their children and even later generations (Richardson et al. 2014).

Besides these new tensions between organismal views of openness, 'plastic' destinies and self-determination on the one side and fixity and 'postgenomic determinism' on the other, the recent return of the organism has also brought an unforeseeable twist to the history of the concept of race in biology. The debate over whether racial categories or differences are biological has a long history, dating back to 18th-century racial classifications by Carl Linnaeus and Johann Friedrich Blumenbach. It continues into the 21st century with population genetics research trying to identify genetic clusters that align with human continental populations (Rosenberg et al. 2002; see also Wills 2017). Due to the various problems going along with this kind of clustering, for a long time historians, social scientists, and philosophers voiced concerns about the centrality of race, for example, in studies of human diversity, the Human Genome Diversity Project, and genetic ancestry testing (M'charek 2005; Tallbear 2013; Lipphardt 2014). They criticized that these approaches distort our understanding of human diversity and lead to stereotyping, othering, and racism.

For these approaches to racial difference, the units of gene and population are crucial. Thus, postgenomics and a shift away from these units to that of the organism should, in principle, hold promise to once and for all abandon biologized views of race and scientific racism in biology. Unfortunately, this assumption is elusive. We currently come to see that new environmental narratives of embodied racial difference emerge from postgenomic biomedical sciences like epigenetics, microbiome research, and DoHaD (for discussion, see Gravlee 2009; Meloni 2017; Saulnier and Dupras 2017; Baedke and Nieves Delgado 2019; Nieves Delgado and Baedke 2021, 2024; Chellappoo and Baedke 2023). Under the new concept of 'biosocial race,' biological differences between races, measured, for example, as differences in groups' DNA-methylation patterns or in the microbial composition of their guts, are now increasingly understood as embodied racial differences. This means that race is no longer defined through intrinsic characteristics of bodies – genes – but through environmentally induced physiological and health-related differences.

For example, in microbiome research, microbial profiles of certain social and ethnic groups are increasingly investigated as embodied racial traits. Here, race is treated as a necessary category that helps in identifying disease susceptibilities and solving health challenges, like type-2 diabetes, in 'western' or Indigenous populations with particular microbial characteristics. Scholars have voiced concerns about this new environmentalist trend to racialize human bodies, as these race studies reinforce outdated historical narratives rooted in colonial stereotypes, are taxonomically problematic and conceptually inconsistent, blur relevant boundaries between the biological and social, and lead to a fragmentation and biologization of social phenomena (e.g., by treating biological states, like microbial composition in the gut or DNA-methylation patterns, as proxies for complex social processes).

As we see, also in the social and anthropological realm the organism concept exerts it influence – albeit a rather ambiguous one. Its recent return in the bio- and biomedical sciences (re)introduces several tensions about how we should understand ourselves as biological units and how we relate to one another and to our environment. First, we see several individualistic and anti-individualistic positions emerging, ranging from an emphasis on autonomy, self-determination, and individual responsibility, to views of social heteronomy and environmental determinism. Second, the shift toward the organism does not overcome problematic super-individual classification patterns, like race. Instead, it helps translating racial classifications into environmentalist versions of race that blur boundaries between social and biological factors and can serve as a new basis for scientific racism.

We should not be too surprised about this facet of the organism concept. In its long history, and especially in the organism-centered biology of the early 20th century, questionable social and political agendas have been closely linked to the organism concept. In fact, ideas of plasticity and agency were often used to legitimize exclusionary and racist positions (see Meloni 2016). One example is German 'Ganzheitsbiologie' and its ties to Nazi ideology (Deichmann 1992; Fábregas-Tejeda et al. 2021; Baedke et al. 2024a). This history tells us that we should reflect more thoroughly on the anthropological and sociopolitical dimensions of the current return of the organism in the bio- and biomedical sciences. A good start for such a project would be to tackle existing ambiguities in the concept that could be exploited by harmful ideologies.

6 Epilogue: The Future of the Organism

Let me conclude by summarizing the results of this investigation of the organism concept and by drawing some general consequences from it. This Element has suggested that we can only understand the role of the organism in biology and beyond, if we integrate historical with philosophical perspectives. It has taken the recent return of the organism in biology as a starting point to reflect on the history of the concept since the 17th century (Section 2) – its origin and rise as arguably the most central concept in biology, and its decline in the second half of the 20th century. I suggested understanding it as a 'nexus concept' that knots together other important concepts. Those associated concepts are the foundation to characterize the organism's internal organizational dimension and its external relational dimension. These two dimensions pay tribute to the two historically grown perspectives in which organisms matter for biologists, as 'organized bodies' and units of interaction. While even today biologists and philosophers mostly foreground only one these two to flesh out the organism concept, and background the other, in this Element I have suggested that we strongly need to start integrating the two in order to finally understand the special causal roles organisms play in nature, especially in developmental evolution. There surely are limitations to this integration (as, e.g., not all organisms can be understood as physiological and evolutionary individuals at the same time), but we should aim for pushing toward these limits and learn to understand them.

As a nexus concept, the organism concept is highly versatile and used in a wide range of biological research. However, this characteristic also creates a problem: integrating several complex concepts can lead to confusion about what the term 'organism' actually refers to. This duality – its versatility and fuzziness – has led, especially in the past 100 years, to alternating phases where organisms have been either emphasized or downplayed in biology. As the most recent representative of such an emphasis, in Section 3, I reviewed the recent return of the organism by looking at new empirical findings and theoretical positions about organisms' plasticity and causal roles in development and evolution. This includes fields like postgenomics, Evo-Devo, epigenetics, niche construction theory and microbiome research, alongside relevant philosophical debates on biological individuality and organismal agency. I identified two long-standing conceptual challenges this recent movement toward the return of the organisms must face: the 'inward challenge' of conceptualizing the organism's unique internal organization and the 'outward challenge' of distinguishing it from its environment, with which it is deeply interlinked.

Then (Section 4), I traced past and present solutions proposed for these challenges. I suggested to look not only at current attempts to establish an organism-centered biology, but also at similar movements in the early 20th century, like organicism and holism. I showed that in both projects the solutions provided show similarities, but also both face serious limitations. Somewhat paradoxically, they often end up in anti-individualistic positions regarding organisms and thus they are at risk of losing this unit as an active and creative agent distinct from other units in nature. In detail, this concerns overemphasizing properties like self-maintenance that organisms share with other systems and neglecting the boundaries between organisms and environments, which are crucial for individuating organisms. To overcome these shortcomings, I proposed a new conceptual framework that not only defines organisms and their boundaries more clearly but also emphasizes their essential agential role in developmental evolution. It, first, expands existing theories of the organizational dimension of organisms by the framework of the 'overcomer,' which highlights organisms as creative agents that control phases of destabilized organization to produce variation. Second, it links this view with the relational dimension of the organism through a model that allows individuating organisms despite their complex reciprocal interactions with the environment. Both arguments together allow securing the role of the organism a special and distinguishable causal nucleus that affects developmental, physiological, ecological, and evolutionary processes.

Finally (Section 5), I explored the sociopolitical and anthropological implications of the nexus concept of the organism. I emphasized how it affects the way we understand ourselves and other humans. Twenty-first century organism-centered biology holds much promise for developing a positive narrative of how we can lead our life in a free and self-determined way, especially as it moves away from gene-centered worldviews. However, at the same time, we need to be on the lookout against new exclusionary and racist frameworks that increasingly build on organismal views. These trends make necessary that biologists and philosophers of biology raise more awareness of the sociopolitical agendas associated with organism-centered biology in the future.

At this point we may ask: What's ahead for the organism in the 21st century? What opportunities and obstacles will determine its future? First, a new organism-centered biology needs to face the fact that the organism concept is one traversed by deep tensions – between inside and outside, organization and relation, individualistic and anti-individualistic views, and even libertarian and deterministic social agendas and worldviews. While the aim to rebuild biology's theoretical foundations on this concept holds much promise for overcoming old epistemic and non-epistemic biases established through narrow gene-centered approaches, one should not expect that the complexity of the organism concept will be easy to handle. Second, the current return of the organism provides many opportunities to complement and rework genetic methodologies with new experimental and field approaches that focus more seriously on different organismal contexts and dynamics. At the same time, this expansion can be challenging as integrating complex data on environmental changes and plasticity into single models can be computationally demanding.

Finally, scientists and philosophers must clarify the epistemic and explanatory standards that organismal accounts should adopt, which will help integrating organism-centered explanations with traditional gene-centered ones in developmental and evolutionary biology. I do not anticipate that organism-centered biology should, in a quasi-Kuhnian manner, replace gene-centered biology. Instead, it should rather expand it, as both serve different, complementary epistemic goals and virtues. Rather than continuing the dialectical back-and-forth of highlighting the organism and replacing it with other causal units, which has dominated the history of biology in the past 100 years, we should finally aim for integrating both perspectives. Indeed, organisms play unique and highly important roles in the processes of life, but they are not the only causal factors. Thus, I think all biologists should learn to deeply and permanently reflect on the influences organisms exert on their chosen research objects, be it genes, populations, or ecosystems. But they surely may focus their research primarily on biological units other than organisms.

Despite these challenges that lie ahead, reestablishing the place of the organism in biology is a worthy endeavor. It is full of promise and rich in history. It may open the door to more pluralist views on biological processes, especially by (re)connecting development and evolution and by overcoming existing research biases. At the same time, there is no straight and clearly marked way forward that is paved by the organism. In fact, the nexus character of the concept does not by itself stipulate a specific theory of organismal organization, clarify how to unambiguously individuate organisms in their environments, or explain how organisms may figure as agents in evolution. Thus, by addressing these issues, this Element has paved the first part of this way. Now it is up to biologists and philosophers to jointly continue this work.

References

Aaby, B. H., and G. Ramsey (2022). "Three Kinds of Niche Construction." *The British Journal for the Philosophy of Science*, 73(2): 351–372.

Allen, C. E., P. Beldade, B. J. Zwaan, et al. (2008). "Differences in the Selection Response of Serially Repeated Color Pattern Characters: Standing Variation, Development, and Evolution." *BMC Evolutionary Biology*, 8(94). https://doi.org/10.1186/1471-2148-8-94.

Allen, G. E. (2005). "Mechanism, Vitalism and Organicism in Late Nineteenth and Twentieth-Century Biology: The Importance of Historical Context." *Studies in History and Philosophy of Science Part C*, 36: 261–283.

Babcock, G., and D. McShea (2024). "Agency as Internal Control." In eds. A. Fábregas-Tejeda, J. Baedke, G. I. Prieto, and G. Radick, *The Riddle of Organismal Agency: New Historical and Philosophical Reflections*, pp. 207–222. Routledge.

Baedke, J. (2017). "The New Biology of the Social: Shaping Humans' Future, Science, and Public Health." In eds. G. Verschraegen, F. Vandermoere, L. Brackmans, and B. Segaert, *Imagined Futures in Science, Technology and Society*, pp. 45–64. Routledge.

(2018). *Above the Gene, Beyond Biology: Towards a Philosophy of Epigenetics*. University of Pittsburgh Press.

(2019a). "O Organism, Where Art Thou? Old and New Challenges for Organism-Centered Biology." *Journal of the History of Biology*, 52(2): 293–324.

(2019b). "What Is a Biological Individual?" In eds. J. M. Martín-Durán, and B. C. Vellutini, *Old Questions and Young Approaches to Animal Evolution (Fascinating Life Sciences)*, pp. 269–284. Springer International.

(2024). "Plant Agency: A Short History from Kant to Plant Psychology, Then to Holism, and Back Again." In eds. A. Fábregas-Tejeda, J. Baedke, G. I. Prieto, and G. Radick, *The Riddle of Organismal Agency: New Historical and Philosophical Reflections*, pp. 62–76. Routledge.

Baedke, J., A. Böhm, and S. Reiners-Selbach (2024a). "From Kant to Holism: The Decline of Neo-Kantianism and the Rise of Theoretical Biology." In eds. H. Pulte, J. Baedke, D. Koenig, and G. Nickel, *New Perspectives on Neo-Kantianism and the Sciences*, pp. 253–277. Routledge.

Baedke, J., A. Böhm, S. Reiners-Selbach, and V. Straetmanns (2024b). "A Synthesis Without Darwin: Unification Attempts in Early Theoretical Biology." In eds. R. G. Delisle, M. Esposito, and D. Ceccarelli, *Unity and*

Disunity in Evolutionary Biology: Deconstructing Darwinism, pp. 333–356. Springer.

Baedke, J., and Ch. Brandt (2022). "Between the Wars, Facing a Scientific Crisis: The Theoretical and Methodological Bottleneck of Interwar Biology (Introduction to Special Issue: New Styles of Thought and Practices: Biology in the Interwar Period)." *Journal of the History of Biology*, 55(2): 209–217.

Baedke, J., and T. Buklijas (2023). "Where Organisms Meet the Environment. Introduction to the Special Issue 'What Counts as Environment in Biology and Medicine: Historical, Philosophical and Sociological Perspectives'." *Studies in History and Philosophy of Science*, 99: A4–A9.

Baedke, J., A. Chellappoo, M. Meloni (2023–2025). "Postgenomic Determinisms: Environmental Narratives after the Century of the Gene." (Topical Collection). *History and Philosophy of the Life Sciences*. https://link .springer.com/collections/ehidceeffb.

Baedke, J. and A. Fábregas-Tejeda (2023). "The Organism in Evolutionary Explanation: From Early 20th Century to the Extended Evolutionary Synthesis." In eds. Th. E. Dickins, and B. J. A. Dickins, *Evolutionary Biology: Contemporary and Historical Reflections Upon Core Theory*, pp. 121–150. Springer.

Baedke, J., A. Fábregas-Tejeda, and A. Nieves Delgado (2020b). "The Holobiont Concept before Margulis." *Journal of Experimental Zoology Part B: Molecular and Developmental Evolution*, 334(3): 149–155.

Baedke, J., A. Fábregas-Tejeda, and G. I. Prieto (2021). "Unknotting Reciprocal Causation between Organism and Environment." *Biology & Philosophy*, 36(5): 48. https://doi.org/10.1007/s10539-021-09815-0.

Baedke, J., A. Fábregas-Tejeda, and F. Vergara-Silva (2020a). "Does the Extended Evolutionary Synthesis Entail Extended Explanatory Power?" *Biology & Philosophy*, 35(1): 20. https://doi.org/10.1007/s10539-020-9736-5.

Baedke, J., and S. F. Gilbert (2024). "Evolution and Development." In ed. E. N. Zalta, *The Stanford Encyclopedia of Philosophy*. (revised 2024 version). https://plato.stanford.edu/archives/fall2020/entries/evolution-development/.

Baedke, J., and A. Nieves Delgado (2019). "Race and Nutrition in the New World: Colonial Shadows in the Age of Epigenetics." *Studies in History and Philosophy of Science Part C: Studies in History and Philosophy of Biological and Biomedical Sciences*, 76(101175). https://doi.org/10.1016/j.shpsc.2019.03.004.

Beckner, M. (1959). *The Biological Way of Thought*. Columbia University Press.

Bechtel, W., and L. Bich (2024). "Situating Homeostasis in Organisms: Maintaining Organization through Time." *The Journal of Physiology*. 602(22): 6003–6020. https://doi.org/10.1113/JP286883.

Bertalanffy, L. v. (1928). *Kritische Theorie der Formbildung*. Borntraeger.

(1932). *Theoretische Biologie, Vol. 1*. Borntraeger.

(1942). *Theoretische Biologie, Vol. 2*. Borntraeger.

Bich, L. (2019). "The Problem of Functional Boundaries in Prebiotic and Inter-Biological Systems." In eds. G. Minati, M. R. Abram, and E. Pessa, *Systemics of Incompleteness and Quasi-Systems*, pp. 295–302. Springer.

Boerhaave, H. (1708). *Institutiones Medicae*. Johannes van der Linden.

(1727). *Historia plantarum*. Francesco Gonzaga.

Bouchard, F., and P. Huneman (2013). *From Groups to Individuals: Perspectives on Biological Associations and Emerging Individuality*. Cambridge University Press.

Buskell, A. (2019). "Reciprocal Causation and the Extended Evolutionary Synthesis." *Biological Theory*, 14: 267–279.

Brooks, D. S. (forthcoming). "The Problem of Organization in Biology and Its Reception in Mainstream Philosophy of Science in the Mid-20th Century." *HOPOS: The Journal of the International Society for the History of Philosophy of Science*.

Canciani, M., Arnellos, A., and A. Moreno (2019). "Revising the Superorganism: An Organizational Approach to Complex Eusociality." *Frontiers in Psychology*, 10(2653). https://doi.org/10.3389/fpsyg.2019.02653.

Charlesworth, D., N. H. Barton, and B. Charlesworth (2017). "The Sources of Adaptive Variation." *Proceedings of the Royal Society B: Biological Sciences*, 284(1855): 20162864. https://doi.org/10.1098/rspb.2016.2864.

Chellappoo, A., and J. Baedke (2023). "Where the Social Meets the Biological: New Ontologies of Biosocial Race." *Synthese*, 201(1): 14.

Cheung, T. (2006). "From the Organism of a Body to the Body of an Organism: Occurrence and Meaning of the Word 'Organism' from the Seventeenth to the Nineteenth Centuries." *British Journal for the History of Science*, 39(3): 319–339.

(2014). *Organismen. Agenten zwischen Innen- und Außenwelten 1780–1860*. Transcript Verlag.

Chiu, L. (2019). "Decoupling, Commingling, and the Evolutionary Significance of Experiential Niche Construction." In eds. T. Uller, Laland, K. N.,

Evolutionary Causation: Biological and Philosophical Reflections, pp. 299–322. MIT Press.

Chiu, L., and S. F. Gilbert (2020). "Niche Construction and the Transition to Herbivory: Phenotype Switching and the Organization of New Nutritional Modes." In eds. H. Levine, M. K. Jolly, P. Kulkarni, V. Nanjundiah, *Phenotypic Switching*, pp. 459–482. Academic Press.

Clark, A. D., D. Deffner, K. Laland, J. Odling-Smee, and J. Endler (2020). "Niche Construction Affects the Variability and Strength of Natural Selection." *The American Naturalist*, 195(1): 16–30.

Clarke, E. (2011). "The Problem of Biological Individuality." *Biological Theory*, 5(4): 312–325.

(2013). "The Multiple Realizability of Biological Individuals." *The Journal of Philosophy*, 110(8): 413–435.

Cummins, R. (1975). "Functional Analysis." *Journal of Philosophy*, 72: 741–765.

Darwin, C. (1859). *On the Origin of Species*. Murray.

Dawkins, R. (1976). *The Selfish Gene*. Oxford University Press.

Deichmann, U. (1992). *Biologen unter Hitler: Vertreibung, Karrieren, Forschung*. Campus-Verlag.

Desmond, H., and P. Huneman (2020). "The Ontology of Organismic Agency: A Kantian Approach." In eds. A. Altobrando, and P. Biasetti, *Natural Born Monads: On the Metaphysics of Organisms and Human Individuals*, pp. 33–64. De Gruyter.

Di Paolo, E. A. (2020). "Picturing Organisms and their Environments: Interaction, Transaction, and Constitution Loops." *Frontiers in Psychology*, 11(1912). https://doi.org/10.3389/fpsyg.2020.01912.

Dobzhansky, T., F. J. Ayala, G. L. Stebbins, and J. W. Valentine (1977). *Evolution*. Freeman.

Dresow, M., and A. C. Love (2023). "Teleonomy: Revisiting a Proposed Conceptual Replacement for Teleology." *Biological Theory*, 18(2): 101–113.

Driesch, H. (1892). "Entwicklungsmechanische Studien. III. Die Verminderung des Furchungsmaterials und ihre Folgen (Weiteres über Theilbildungen). IV. Experimentelle Veränderungen des Typus der Furchung und ihre Folgen (Wirkungen von Wärmezufuhr und von Druck). V. Von der Furchung doppeltbefruchteter Eier. VI. Ueber einige allgemeine Fragen der theoretischen Morphologie." *Zeitschrift für wissenschaftliche Zoologie*, 55: 1–62.

Dupré, J., and M. A. O'Malley (2009). "Varieties of living things: Life at the intersection of lineage and metabolism." *Philosophy and Theory in Biology*, I: e003. http://dx.doi.org/10.3998/ptb.6959004.0001.003.

Echelard-Dumas, M. (1976). "Der Begriff des Organismus bei Leibniz: 'Biologische Tatsache' und Fundierung." *Studia Leibnitiana*, 8: 160–186.

Edelaar, P., J. Otsuka, and V. J. Luque (2023). "A Generalised Approach to the Study and Understanding of Adaptive Evolution." *Biological Reviews*, 98(1): 352–375.

El-Hani, C. N., F. R. G. de Lima, and N. de F. Nunes-Neto (2024). "From the Organizational Theory of Ecological Functions to a New Notion of Sustainability." In ed. M. Mossio, *Organization in Biology*, pp. 285–328. Springer.

Esposito, M. (2016). *Romantic Biology, 1890–1945*. Routledge.

Fábregas-Tejeda, A. (2024). "Charting Contrasting Stances on Organismal Purposiveness and Agency in Early Twentieth-Century Biology." In eds. A. Fábregas-Tejeda, J. Baedke, G. I. Prieto, and G. Radick, *The Riddle of Organismal Agency*, pp. 41–60. Routledge.

(forthcoming). *The Organism-Environment Pairing: A Historical and Philosophical Re-Appraisal*. MIT Press.

Fábregas-Tejeda, A., J. Baedke, G. I. Prieto, and G. Radick (eds.) (2024). *The Riddle of Organismal Agency: New Historical and Philosophical Reflections*. Routledge.

Fábregas-Tejeda, A., A. Nieves Delgado, and J. Baedke (2021). "Revisiting Hans Böker's 'Species Transformation through Reconstruction: Reconstruction through Active Reaction of Organisms' (1935)." *Biological Theory*, 16: 63–75.

Fábregas-Tejeda, A., and F. Vergara-Silva (2018). "The Emerging Structure of the Extended Evolutionary Synthesis: Where Does Evo-Devo Fit in?" *Theory in Biosciences*, 52: 169–184.

Falconer, D. S. (1960). *Introduction to Quantitative Genetics*. Ronald Press.

Fitz-James, M. H., and G. Cavalli (2022). "Molecular Mechanisms of Transgenerational Epigenetic Inheritance." *Nature Reviews Genetics*, 23: 325–341.

Folse III, H. J., and J. Roughgarden, (2010). "What Is an iIndividual Organism? A Multilevel Selection Perspective." *The Quarterly Review of Biology*, 85(4): 447–472.

Forde, B. G. (2009). "Is It Good Noise? The Role of Developmental Instability in the Shaping of a Root System." *Journal of Experimental Botany*, 60(14): 3989–4002.

Gardner, A., and A. Grafen (2009). "Capturing the Superorganism: A Formal Theory of Group Adaptation." *Journal of Evolutionary Biology*, 22: 659–671.

Gassendi, P. (1658). *Syntagma Philosophicum (Opera omnia, Vol. 2)*. Anisson & Devenet.

Gierer, A. (1996). "Organisms-Mechanisms: Stahl, Wolff and the Case against Reductionist Exclusion." *Science in Context*, 9: 511–530.

Gilbert, S. F. (2014). "A Bolobiont Birth Narrative: The Epigenetic Transmission of the Human Microbiome." *Frontiers in Genetics*, 5(282). https://doi.org/10.3389/fgene.2014.00282.

Gilbert, S. F. (2020). "Developmental Symbiosis Facilitates the Multiple Origins of Herbivory." *Evolution & Development*, 22(1–2): 154–164.

Gilbert, S. F., D. Epel (2015). *Ecological Developmental Biology*. 2nd ed. Sinauer.

Gilbert, S. F., J. Sapp, A. I. Tauber (2012). "A Symbiotic View of Life: We Have Never Been Individuals." *The Quarterly Review of Biology*, 87: 325–341.

Giroux, É., F. Merlin, and Y. Fayet (2023). *Integrative Approaches in Environmental Health and Exposome Research: Epistemological and Practical Issues*. Springer Nature.

Godfrey-Smith, P. (2013). "Darwinian Individuals." In eds. F. Bouchard, and P. Huneman, *From Groups to Individuals: Evolution and Emerging Individuality*, pp. 17–36. MIT Press.

Goodwin, B. (1999). "Reclaiming a Life of Quality." *Journal of Consciousness Studies*, 6: 229–235.

Gould, S. J. (1980). "Is a New and General Theory of Evolution Emerging?" *Paleobiology*, 6: 119–130.

Gravlee, C. C. (2009). "How Race Becomes Biology: Embodiment of Social Inequality." *American Journal of Physical Anthropology*, 139: 47–57.

Griffiths, P. E., R. D. Gray (2001). "Darwinism and developmental systems." In eds. S. Oyama, P. E. Griffiths, R. D. Gray, *Cycles of Contingency*, pp. 195–218. MIT Press.

Guttinger, S., and J. Dupré (2016). "Genomics and Postgenomics." In ed. E. N. Zalta, *The Stanford Encyclopedia of Philosophy*. https://plato.stan ford.edu/entries/genomics/.

Haldane, J. S. (1884). "Life and Mechanism." *Mind*, 9: 27–47.

(1917). *Organism and Environment as Illustrated by the Physiology of Breathing*. Yale University Press.

(1935). *The Philosophy of a Biologist*. Claredon.

Haraway, D. J. (2004). *Crystal, Fabrics, and Fields: Metaphors that Shape Embryos*. North Atlantic Books. [Original 1976].

Harwood, J. (1993). *Styles of Scientific Thought: The German Genetics Community, 1900–1933*. University of Chicago Press.

Hazelwood, C. (2023). "Reciprocal Causation and Biological Practice." *Biology & Philosophy*, 38(1): 5. https://doi.org/10.1007/s10539-023-09895-0.

Hertwig, O. (1922). *Der Staat als Organismus: Gedanken zur Entwicklung der Menschheit*. G. Fischer.

Hull, D. L. (1980). "Individuality and Selection." *Annual Review of Ecology and Systematics*, 11: 311–332.

Huneman, P. (2010). "Assessing the Prospects for a Return of Organisms in Evolutionary Biology." *History and Philosophy of the Life Sciences*, 32: 341–371.

(2021). "Biological Individuals as "Weak Individuals" and their Identity: Exploring a Radical Hypothesis in the Metaphysics of Science." In eds. A. S. Meincke, and J. Dupré, *Biological Identity: Perspectives from Metaphysics and the Philosophy of Biology*, pp. 40–62. Routledge.

Huneman, P., and D. Walsh (2017). *Challenging the Synthesis: Adaptation, Development, Inheritance*. Oxford University Press.

Jablonka, E., and M. J. Lamb (2014). *Evolution in Four Dimensions: Genetic, Epigenetic, Behavioral, and Symbolic Variation in the History of Life*. 2nd ed. MIT Press.

(2020). *Inheritance Systems and the Extended Synthesis*. Cambridge University Press.

Jaeger, J. (2024). "The Fourth Perspective: Evolution and Organismal Agency." In ed. M. Mossio, *Organization in Biology*, pp. 159–186. Springer International.

Jacob, F. (1977). "Evolution and Tinkering." *Science*, 196(4295): 1161–1166.

Jokura, K., T. Anttonen, M. Rodriguez-Santiago, and O. M. Arenas (2024). "Rapid Physiological Integration of Fused Ctenophores." *Current Biology*, 34(19): R889–890.

Jones, C. G., J. H. Lawton, and M. Shachak (1994). "Organisms as Ecosystem Engineers." *Oikos*, 69: 373–386.

Kaiser, M. I., and R. Trappes (2021). "Broadening the Problem Agenda of Biological Individuality: Individual Differences, Uniqueness and Temporality." *Biology & Philosophy*, 36(2): 15. https://doi.org/10.1007/s10539-021-09791-5.

Kant, I. (1913) "Kritik der Urtheilskraft." In ed. Königlich Preußische Akademie der Wissenschaften, *Kant's gesammelte Schriften, Vol. 5.*, pp. 165–485. Reimer. [Original 1790/93].

Keller, E. F. (2000). *The Century of the Gene*. Harvard University Press.

Khan, I., A. Prakash, and D. Agashe (2016). "Divergent Immune Priming Responses across Flour Beetle Life Stages and Populations." *Ecology and Evolution*, 6(21): 7847–7855.

Kimura, I., J. Miyamoto, R. Ohue-Kitano, et al. (2020). "Maternal Gut Microbiota in Pregnancy Influences Offspring Metabolic Phenotype in Mice." *Science*, 367(6481): eaaw8429. https://doi.org/10.1126/science.aaw8429.

Kingma, E. (2020). "Biological Individuality, Pregnancy, and (Mammalian) Reproduction." *Philosophy of Science*, 87: 1037–1048.

Köchy, K. (1997). *Ganzheit und Wissenschaft. Das historische Fallbeispiel der romantischen Naturforschung.* Königshausen and Neumann.

Lala, K. N., T. Uller, N. Feiner, M. Feldman, and S. F. Gilbert (2024). *Evolution Evolving: The Developmental Origins of Adaptation and Biodiversity.* Princeton University Press.

Laland, K., and G. Brown (2018). "The Social Construction of Human Nature." In eds. T. Lewens, E. Hannon, *Why We Disagree About Human Nature*, pp. 127–144. Oxford University Press.

Laland, K. N., J. Odling-Smee, M. W. Feldman (2019). "Understanding Niche Construction as an Evolutionary Process." In eds. T. Uller, K. N. Laland, *Evolutionary Causation*, pp. 127–152. MIT Press.

Laland, K. N., T. Uller, M. W. Feldman, et al. (2014). "Does Evolutionary Theory Need a Rethink? Yes, urgently." *Nature News*, 514: 161–164.

Laland, K. N., T. Uller, M. W. Feldman, et al. (2015). "The Extended Evolutionary Synthesis: Its Structure, Assumptions and Predictions." *Proceedings of the Royal Society B*, 282(1813): 20151019. https://doi.org/10.1098/rspb.2015.1019.

Laubichler, M. D. (2017). "The Emergence of Theoretical and General Biology: The Broader Scientific Context for the Biologische Versuchsanstalt." In ed. G. B. Müller, *Vivarium: Experimental, Quantitative, and Theoretical Biology at Vienna's Biologische Versuchsanstalt*, pp. 95–114. MIT Press.

Lenoir, T. (1982). *The Strategy of Life: Teleology and Mechanics in Nineteenth Century German Biology.* Reidel.

Levins, R., and R. C. Lewontin (1985). *The Dialectical Biologist.* Harvard University Press.

Lewontin, R. C. (1982). "Organism and Environment." In ed. H. C. Plotkin, *Learning, Development, and Culture*, pp. 151–170. Wiley.

Lidgard, S., and L. K. Nyhart (2017). *Biological Individuality: Integrating Scientific, Philosophical, and Historical Perspectives.* University of Chicago Press.

Lipphardt, V. (2014). "Geographical Distribution Patterns of Various Genes: Genetic Studies of Human Variation after 1945." *Studies in History and Philosophy of Science Part C*, 47: 50–61.

Lo, L. K., N. K. Schulz, H. Jensen, and J. Kurtz (2025). Experimental Removal of Niche Construction Alters the Pace and Mechanisms of Resistance Evolution. Preprint. https://doi.org/10.1101/2025.03.27.645637.

Lohse, S. (2023). "Mapping Uncertainty in Precision Medicine: A Systematic Scoping Review." *Journal of Evaluation in Clinical Practice*, 29: 554–564.

Loison, L. (2024). *Beyond Lamarckism: Plasticity in Darwinian Evolution, 1890–1970*. Taylor & Francis.

Lorenz, K. Z. (1966). *On Aggression*. Harcourt, Brace and World.

Maturana, H. R., and F. J. Varela (1980). *Autopoiesis and Cognition: The Realization of the Living*. Springer. [Original 1972].

Mayr, E. (1961). "Cause and Effect in Biology." *Science*, 134: 1501–1506.

(1985). "Teleological and Teleonomic: A New Analysis." In eds. R. S. Cohen, M. W. Wartofsky, *A Portrait of Twenty-five Years: Boston Colloquium for the Philosophy of Science 1960–1985*, pp. 133–159. Reidel. [Original 1974].

M'charek, A. (2005). *The Human Genome Diversity Project: An Ethnography of Scientific Practice*. Cambridge University Press.

McConwell, A. K. (2023). *Biological Individuality*. Cambridge University Press.

McLaughlin, M. (2012). "Babies Born into Poverty are Damaged Forever before Birth." *The Scotsman*, (January 24). www.scotsman.com/news/babies-born-into-poverty-are-damaged-forever-before-birth-2465469. [Accessed 05 Oct 2024].

Meloni, M. (2017). "Race in an Epigenetic Time: Thinking Biology in the Plural." *The British Journal of Sociology*, 68(3): 389–409.

Merlin, F., and É. Giroux (2024). "Narratives in Exposomics: A Reversed Heuristic Determinism?" *History and Philosophy of the Life Sciences*, 46(22). https://doi.org/10.1007/s40656-024-00620-y.

Mesoudi, A., S. A. Blanchet, A. Charmantier, et al (2013). "Is Non-genetic Inheritance Just a Proximate Mechanism? A Corroboration of the Extended Evolutionary Synthesis." *Biological Theory*, 7: 189–195.

Meyer-Abich, A. (1955). "Organismen als Holismen." *Acta Biotheoretica*, 11(2): 85–106.

Minelli, A. (2009). *Forms of Becoming: The Evolutionary Biology of Development*. Princeton University Press.

Mitoh, S., and Y. Yusa (2021). "Extreme Autotomy and Whole-Body Regeneration in Photosynthetic Sea Slugs." *Current Biology*, 31(5): R233–234.

Moczek, A. P. (2015). "Re-evaluating the Environment in Developmental Evolution." *Frontiers in Ecology and Evolution*, 3(7). https://doi.org/10.3389/fevo.2015.00007.

Monod, J. (1971). *Chance and Necessity: An Essay on the Natural Philosophy of Modern Biology.* Alfred A. Knopf.

Montévil, M., M. Mossio, A. Pocheville, and G. Longo (2016). "Theoretical Principles for Biology: Variation." *Progress in Biophysics and Molecular Biology*, 122(1): 36–50.

Moreno, A., and M. Mossio (2015). *Biological Autonomy: A Philosophical and Theoretical Enquiry.* Springer.

Morgan, T. H. (1910). "Sex Limited Inheritance in Drosophila." *Science*, 32: 120–122.

Moss, L. (2001). "Deconstructing the Gene and Reconstructing Molecular Developmental Systems." In eds. S. Oyama, P. E. Griffiths, and R. D. Gray, *Cycles of Contingency: Developmental Systems and Evolution*, pp. 85–98. MIT Press.

Mossio, M. (2024). "Introduction: Organization as a Scientific Blind Spot." In ed. M. Mossio, *Organization in Biology*, pp. 1–22. Springer International.

Mossio, M., and L. Bich (2017). "What Makes Biological Organisation Teleological?" *Synthese*, 194(4): 1089–1114.

Mossio, M., M. Montévil, and G. Longo (2016). "Theoretical Principles for Biology: Organization." *Progress in Biophysics and Molecular Biology, from the Century of the Genome to the Century of the Organism: New Theoretical Approaches*, 122(1): 24–35.

Mossio, M., and A. Moreno (2010). "Organisational Closure in Biological Organisms." *History and Philosophy of the Life Sciences*, 32: 269–288.

Müller, G. B. (2017). "Why an Extended Evolutionary Synthesis Is Necessary." *Interface Focus*, 7(5): 20170015. https://doi.org/10.1098/rsfs.2017.0015.

(2024). "The Epigenetic System, Evo-devo, and the Extended Evolutionary Synthesis." In ed. C. M. Guerrero-Bosagna, *On Epigenetics and Evolution*, pp. 1515–40. Academic Press.

Nagel, E. (1951). "Mechanistic Explanation and Organismic Biology." *Philosophy and Phenomenological Research*, 11(3): 327–338.

Nahas, A. (2024). "Behavior, Purpose, and Teleology Revisited: Locating Cybernetic Teleology in Twentieth- Century Holism." In eds. A. Fábregas-Tejeda, J. Baedke, G. I. Prieto, and G. Radick, *The Riddle of Organismal Agency*, pp. 77–94. Routledge.

Nahas, A., and C. Sachs (2023). "What's at Stake in the Debate over Naturalizing Teleology? An Overlooked Metatheoretical Debate." *Synthese*, 201(4): 142. doi.org/10.1007/s11229-023-04147-w.

Nakagawa, S., D. W. Armitage, T. Froese, Y. Yang, and M. Lagisz (2025). "Poor Hypotheses and Research Waste in Biology: Learning from a Theory Crisis in Psychology." *BMC Biology*, 23(1): 33. https://doi.org/10.1186/s12915-025-02134-w.

Neander, K. (1991). "The Teleological Notion of 'Function'." *Australasian Journal of Philosophy*, 69(4): 454–468.

Needham, J. (1936). *Order and Life*. Yale University Press.

Nicholson, D. J. (2014). "The Return of the Organism as a Fundamental Explanatory Concept in Biology." *Philosophy Compass*, 9: 347–359.

(2018). "Reconceptualizing the Organism: From Complex Machine to Flowing Stream." In eds. J. Dupré, D. J. Nicholson, *Everything Flows*, pp. 139–166. Oxford University Press.

Nicholson, D. J., and R. Gawne (2014). "Rethinking Woodger's Legacy in the Philosophy of Biology." *Journal of the History of Biology*, 47: 243–292.

(2015). "Neither Logical Empiricism nor Vitalism, but Organicism: What the Philosophy of Biology Was." *History and Philosophy of the Life Sciences*, 37: 345–381.

Nieves Delgado, A., and J. Baedke (2021). "Does the Human Microbiome Tell Us Something about Race?" *Humanities and Social Sciences Communications*, 8: 1–12.

(2024). "How to Eliminate Race from Human Microbiome Research." *Argumenta*, 1–14.

Niewöhner, J. (2011). "Epigenetics: Embedded Bodies and the Molecularisation of Biography and Milieu." *BioSocieties*, 6: 279–298.

Nicoglou, A. (2024). *Plasticity in the Life Sciences*. University of Chicago Press.

Nuche, P., B. Komac, J. J. Camarero, and C. L. Alados (2014). "Developmental Instability as an Index of Adaptation to Drought Stress in a Mediterranean Oak." *Ecological Indicators*, 40(May): 68–75.

Nunes-Neto, N., A. Moreno, A., and C. N. El-Hani (2014). "Function in Ecology: An Organizational Approach." *Biology & Philosophy*, 29: 123–141.

Odling-Smee, J. (2024). *Niche Construction: How Life Contributes to Its Own Evolution*. MIT Press.

Odling-Smee, F. J., K. N. Laland, and M. W. Feldman (2003). *Niche Construction: The Neglected Process in Evolution*. Princeton University Press.

Okasha, S. (2018). *Agents and Goals in Evolution*. Oxford University Press.
(forthcoming). "On the Very Idea of Biological Individuality." *British Journal for the Philosophy of Science*. https://doi.org/10.1086/728048.

Otsuka, J. (2015). "Using Causal Models to Integrate Proximate and Ultimate Causation." *Biology & Philosophy*, 30: 19–37.

Oyama, S. (2000). "Causal Democracy and Causal Contributions in Developmental Systems Theory." *Philosophy of Science*, 67(S3): S332–S347.

Pearce, T. (2020). *Pragmatism's Evolution: Organism and Environment in American Philosophy*. University of Chicago Press.

Penick, C. A., M. Ghaninia, K. L. Haight, et al (2021). "Reversible Plasticity in Brain Size, Behaviour and Physiology Characterizes Caste Transitions in a Socially Flexible Ant (Harpegnathos Saltator)." *Proceedings of the Royal Society B: Biological Sciences*, 288(1948): 20210141. https://doi.org/10.1098/rspb.2021.0141.

Peterson, E. L. (2016). *The Life Organic: The Theoretical Biology Club and the Roots of Epigenetics*. University of Pittsburgh Press.

Piaget, J. (1976). *La Comportement Moteur de l'Evolution*. Gallimard.

Pietsch, Th. W. (2009). *Oceanic Anglerfishes: Extraordinary Diversity in the Deep Sea*. University of California Press.

Pickersgill, M., J. Niewöhner, R. Müller, P. Martin, and S. Cunningham-Burley (2013). "Mapping the New Molecular Landscape: Social Dimensions of Epigenetics." *New Genetics and Society*, 32(4): 429–447.

Pigliucci, M., and G. B. Müller (eds.) (2010). *Evolution: The Extended Synthesis*. MIT Press.

Pittendrigh, C. S. (1958). "Adaptation, Natural Selection, and Behavior." In eds. A. Roe, G. G. Simpson, *Behavior and Evolution*, pp. 390–416. Yale University Press.

Polak, M. (ed.) (2003). *Developmental Instability: Causes and Consequences*. Oxford University Press.

Pradeu, T. (2010). "What is an Organism? An Immunological Answer." *History and Philosophy of the Life Sciences*, 32: 247–267.
(2016). "Organisms or Biological Individuals? Combining Physiological and Evolutionary Individuality." *Biology & Philosophy*, 31: 797–817.

Prieto, G. I. (2023): "'Organism' versus 'Biological Individual': The Missing Demarcation." *ArtefaCToS. Revista de estudios sobre la ciencia y la tecnología*, 12(1): 27–54. http://doi.org/10.14201/art20231212754.
(2024). *Organisms and Biological Individuals: A Bio-Philosophical Inquiry*. Dissertation. Ruhr University Bochum.

Richardson, S. S., C. R. Daniels, M. W. Gillman, et al (2014). "Society: Don't Blame the Mothers." *Nature News*, 512(7513): 131–132.

Richardson, S. S., and H. Stevens (2015). *Postgenomics: Perspectives on Biology after the Genome*. Duke University Press.

Rickert, H. (1902). *Die Grenzen der naturwissenschaftlichen Begriffsbildung: Eine logische Einleitung in die historischen Wissenschaften*. Mohr.

Riskin, J. (2016). *The Restless Clock: A History of the Centuries-Long Argument Over What Makes Living Things Tick*. University of Chicago Press.

Ritter, W. E. (1919). *The Unity of the Organism, or the Organismal Conception of Life, 2 Vols*. Gorham Press.

Rosenberg, N. A., J. K. Pritchard, H. M. Weber, et al. (2002). "Genetic Structure of Human Populations." *Science*, 298: 2381–2385.

Roughgarden, J., S. F. Gilbert, E. Rosenberg, et al. (2018). "Holobionts as Units of Selection and a Model of their Population Dynamics and Evolution." *Biological Theory*, 13: 44–65.

Rupik, G. (2024). *Remapping Biology with Goethe, Schelling, and Herder: Romanticizing Evolution*. Routledge.

Russell, E. S. (1930). *The Interpretation of Development and Heredity*. Clarendon Press.

(1950). "The 'Drive' Element in Life." *The British Journal for the Philosophy of Science*, 1: 108–116.

Sankar, P. L., and L. S. Parker (2017). "The Precision Medicine Initiative's All of Us Research Program: An Agenda for Research on Its Ethical, Legal, and Social Issues." *Genetics in Medicine*, 19(7): 743–750.

Saulnier, K. M., and C. Dupras (2017). "Race in the Postgenomic Era: Social Epigenetics Calling for Interdisciplinary Ethical Safeguards." *American Journal of Bioethics*, 17: 58–60.

Schaxel, J. (1919). *Grundzüge der Theoriebildung in der Biologie*. Fischer.

Schrödinger, E. (1944). *What is Life?* Macmillan.

Shiroyama, H., S. Mitoh, Y. I. Takashi, and Y. Yusa (2020). "Adaptive Significance of Light and Food for a Kleptoplastic Sea Slug: Implications for Photosynthesis." *Oecologia*, 194(3): 455–463.

Shtein, I., A. Koyfman, A. Eshel, and B. Bar-On (2019). "Autotomy in Plants: Organ Sacrifice in Oxalis Leaves." *Journal of the Royal Society Interface*, 16(151). https://doi.org/10.1098/rsif.2018.0737.

Smith, S. E. (2017). "Organisms as Persisters." *Philosophy, Theory, and Practice in Biology*, 9(14). https://doi.org/10.3998/ptb.6959004.0009.014.

Spemann, H., and H. Mangold (1924). "Über Induktion von Embryonalanlagen durch Implantation artfremder Organisatoren." *Archiv für mikroskopische Anatomie und Entwicklungsmechanik*, 100: 599–638.

Stahl, G. E. (1684). *Dissertatio medica inauguralis de intestinis eorumque morbis ac symptomatis cognoscendis et curandis*. University Jena.

Steigerwald, J. (2019). *Experimenting at the Boundaries of Life: Organic Vitality in Germany around 1800*. University of Pittsburgh Press.

Stotz, K. (2008). "The Ingredients for a Postgenomic Synthesis of Nature and Nurture." *Philosophical Psychology*, 21: 359–381.

Suárez, J. (2020). "The Stability of Traits Conception of the Hologenome: An Evolutionary Account of Holobiont Individuality." *History and Philosophy of the Life Sciences*, 42(1): 11. https://doi.org/10.1007/s40656-020-00305-2.

Sultan, S. E. (2015). *Organism and Environment: Ecological Development, Niche Construction, and Adaptation*. Oxford University Press.

Sultan, S. E., A. P. Moczek, and D. Walsh (2022). "Bridging the Explanatory Gaps: What Can We Learn from a Biological Agency Perspective?" *BioEssays*, 44(1): 2100185. https://doi.org/10.1002/bies.202100185.

Swann, J. B., S. J. Holland, M. Petersen, Th. W. Pietsch, and Th. Boehm (2020). "The Immunogenetics of Sexual Parasitism." *Science*, 369(6511): 1608–1615.

Tallbear, K. (2013). *Native American DNA: Tribal Belonging and the False Promise of Genetic Science*. University of Minnesota Press.

Toepfer, G. (2011). "Organismus." In ed. G. Toepfer, *Historisches Wörterbuch der Biologie, Vol. 2.*, pp. 777–842. Metzler.

  (2012). "Teleology and Its Constitutive Role for Biology as the Science of Organized Systems in Nature." *Studies in History and Philosophy of Science Part C*, 43: 113–119.

  (2024). "Philosophy of Biology in Neo-Kantianism." In eds. H. Pulte, J. Baedke, D. Koenig, and G. Nickel, *New Perspectives on Neo-Kantianism and the Sciences*, pp. 215–231. Routledge.

Uexküll, J. v. (1909). *Umwelt und Innenwelt der Tiere*. Springer.

  (1922). "Technische und mechanische Biologie." *Ergebnisse der Physiologie*, 20: 129–161.

  (1928). *Theoretische Biologie*. 2nd ed. Springer.

Virenque, L., and M. Mossio (2024). "What Is Agency? A View from Autonomy Theory." *Biological Theory*, 19(1): 11–15.

Waddington, C. H. (1957). *The Strategy of the Genes: A Discussion of Some Aspects of Theoretical Biology*. Allen & Unwin.

(1959). "Evolutionary Systems–Animal and Human." *Nature*, 183: 1634–1638.

(1960). "Evolutionary Adaptation." In ed. S. Tax, *Evolution after Darwin*, pp. 381–402. University of Chicago Press.

Waggoner, M. R., and T. Uller (2015). "Epigenetic Determinism in Science and Society." *New Genetics and Society*, 34(2): 177–195.

Wagner, A. (2014). *Arrival of the Fittest: Solving Evolution's Greatest Puzzle.* Penguin.

Walsh, D. M. (2015). *Organisms, Agency, and Evolution.* Cambridge University Press.

(2017). "Chance Caught on the Wing: Metaphysical Commitment or Methodological Artifact?" In eds. P. Huneman, and D. Walsh, *Challenging the Synthesis: Adaptation, Development, Inheritance*, pp. 239–261. Oxford University Press.

(2019). "The Paradox of Population Thinking: First Order Causes and High Order Effects." In eds. T. Uller, and K. Laland, *Evolutionary Causation: Biological and Philosophical Reflections*, pp. 227–246. MIT Press.

(2021). "Aristotle and Contemporary Biology." In ed. S. M. Connell, *The Cambridge Companion to Aristotle's Biology*, pp. 280–297. Cambridge University Press.

(2022). "Environment as Abstraction." *Biological Theory*, 17: 68–79.

Walsh, D. M., and S. E. Sultan (2024). "The Higher-Order Norm of Reaction: Biological Agency and Adaptive Phenotypic Response." In eds. A. Fábregas-Tejeda, J. Baedke, G. I. Prieto, and G. Radick, *The Riddle of Organismal Agency*, pp. 114–130. Routledge.

Weiss, P. A. (1969). "The Living System: Determinism Stratified." In eds. A. Koestler and J. Raymond Smythies, *Beyond Reductionism: New Perspectives in the Life Sciences*, pp. 3–55. Hutchinson.

West-Eberhard, M. J. (2003). *Developmental Plasticity and Evolution.* Oxford University Press.

(2005). "Developmental Plasticity and the Origin of Species Differences." *Proceedings of the National Academy of Sciences*, 102: 6543–6549.

Wills, M. (2017). "Are Clusters Races? A Discussion of the Rhetorical Appropriation of Rosenberg et al.'s 'Genetic Structure of Human Populations.'" *Philosophy & Theory in Biology*, 9(12). http://dx.doi.org/10.3998/ptb.6959004.0009.012.

Wheeler, W. M. (1911). "The Ant Colony as an Organism." *Journal of Morphology*, 22: 307–325.

Whitehead, A. N. (1925). *Science and the Modern World.* Macmillan Company.

Williams, G. C. (1992). "Gaia, Nature Worship and Biocentric Fallacies." *The Quarterly Review of Biology*, 67: 479–486.

Wimsatt, W. C. (1971). "Function, Organization, and Selection." *Zygon*, 6: 168–172.

(1974). "Complexity and Organization." In eds. K. F. Schaffner and R. S. Cohen, *PSA 1972: Proceedings of the Biennial Meeting of the Philosophy of Science Association*, pp. 67–86. University of Chicago Press.

Woodger, J. H. (1929). *Biological Principles*. Routledge and Kegan Paul.

Woodward, J. (2003). *Making Things Happen*. Oxford University Press.

Zhang, B., S. P. Leonard, Y. Li, and N. A. Moran (2019). "Obligate Bacterial Endosymbionts Limit Thermal Tolerance of Insect Host Species." *Proceedings of the National Academy of Sciences*, 116(49): 24712–24718.

Acknowledgments

I want to thank Alejandro Fábregas-Tejeda, Guido Prieto, Daniel Brooks, Abigail Nieves Delgado, Denis Walsh, and an anonymous reviewer for constructive comments on different versions of the manuscript and for discussions of ideas leading toward this Element, and Friederike Andrae, who helped formatting the manuscript. The work on this Element was financially supported by the German Research Foundation (DFG), Project "The Return of the Organism in the Biosciences: Theoretical, Historical, and Social Dimensions" (Emmy Noether Group, no. BA5808/2–1). Besides that, the ideas developed in these pages were discussed and sharpened at various conferences, among others, the Meetings of the International Society for the History, Philosophy, and Social Studies of Biology (ISHPSSB; 2017, 2019), the Meeting of the History of Science Society (HHS; 2019), the Meeting of the European Society for History of Science (ESHS; 2020), and the Meeting of the European Society of Philosophy of Science (EPSA, 2021). I thank session participants for helpful comments. Finally, I am grateful to my editors Grant Ramsey and Michael Ruse for their enthusiasm in the project.

Cambridge Elements ≡

Philosophy of Biology

Grant Ramsey
KU Leuven

Grant Ramsey is a BOFZAP research professor at the Institute of Philosophy, KU Leuven, Belgium. His work centers on philosophical problems at the foundation of evolutionary biology. He has been awarded the Popper Prize twice for his work in this area. He also publishes in the philosophy of animal behavior, human nature and the moral emotions. He runs the Ramsey Lab (theramseylab.org), a highly collaborative research group focused on issues in the philosophy of the life sciences.

About the Series

This Cambridge Elements series provides concise and structured introductions to all of the central topics in the philosophy of biology. Contributors to the series are cutting-edge researchers who offer balanced, comprehensive coverage of multiple perspectives, while also developing new ideas and arguments from a unique viewpoint.

9 781009 495066